THE UNAPOLOGETIC PROFESSIONAL

How to Lead, Create, and Succeed
Without Shrinking Yourself to
Fit the Mold

BRIANNA DOE

WILEY

Published by John Wiley & Sons, Inc., Hoboken, New Jersey.
Published simultaneously in Canada.

For general information on our other products and services or for technical support, please contact our Customer Care Department within the United States at (800) 762-2974, outside the United States at (317) 572-3993 or fax (317) 572-4002.

Wiley also publishes its books in a variety of electronic formats. Some content that appears in print may not be available in electronic formats. For more information about Wiley products, visit our web site at www.wiley.com.

Library of Congress Cataloging-in-Publication Data:

Names: Doe, Brianna, author.
Title: The unapologetic professional : how to lead, create, and succeed without
     shrinking yourself to fit the mold
     / Brianna Doe.
Description: Hoboken, New Jersey : Wiley, [2026] | Includes bibliographical
     references and index.
Identifiers: LCCN 2025032289 | ISBN 9781394329441 (hardback) | ISBN
     9781394329465 (adobe pdf) | ISBN 9781394329458 (epub)
Subjects: LCSH: Vocational guidance. | Success.
Classification: LCC HF5381 .D64 2026
LC record available at https://lccn.loc.gov/2025032289

Cover Design: Brianna Doe

Set in 11/16pt ITCGaramondStd-Lt by Lumina Datamatics

SKY10126330_091225

To my uncle Winston, who always made his quiet, curious, slightly offbeat niece feel seen and special. Thank you for indulging my endless questions about the world and for never making me feel like I was "too much."

And to my grandma Winnie, who bravely packed up three kids and left Jamaica for Brooklyn, working long hours and raising them on her own. Your strength lives on in your daughter, grandchildren, and great-granddaughters.

You are both missed. Every day.

Contents

Contents

About the Author

Brianna Doe is an award-winning marketer, writer, speaker, and content strategist with 14 years of experience leading high-impact marketing programs across tech, sports, politics, fashion, and more. A 3x entrepreneur, she's built influencer activations for both household names and startups alike. Her work sits at the intersection of culture, identity, and the unglamorous reality of building something from scratch. And she's not afraid to say the quiet part out loud.

Brianna regularly writes and speaks about entrepreneurship, leadership, marketing, the future of work, and how to navigate all of it without losing yourself in the process. Her work has been featured by Fast Company, CNBC, Business Insider, and the American Marketing Association.

If she's not writing, speaking, or working with influencers, she's probably watching horror movies, planning her next tattoo, or planning her next trip (preferably somewhere warm and walkable). She lives in Phoenix with her husband and their two extremely photogenic dogs, Rocket and Nova.

Acknowledgments

This book was written during one of the busiest, most chaotic, most beautiful chapters of my life. I was planning my wedding, building a business, hopping on way too many flights, and rewriting chapters in hotel lobbies, Lyfts, and the occasional airport bar. It would've been easy to fall apart or lose focus. But thanks to the people in the next few lines, I didn't.

So, thank you:

To Michael—my husband, my partner, my steady-in-the-storm. I don't know how you managed to stay so calm while I was spiraling about chapter titles and deadlines. You have been my rock through every late night, every rewrite, every 3 a.m. writing session I swore would "only take an hour." I'm endlessly grateful I get to do life with you.

To my mom, who let me fill notebook after notebook with stories, tall tales, and whatever my imagination cooked up. I might doubt myself constantly, but you never have. Every time I hit a milestone, you act like you've just been waiting for the rest of the world to catch up. Thank you for always reminding me who I am.

To my brother Abraham and sister-in-law Alicia, for being my biggest cheerleaders, even when I'm not around to hear it. Knowing that you, Lydia, and Jasmine are in my corner means more than you probably realize.

To Devon Adams, Liza Sejkora, and every teacher and professor who encouraged and cultivated my love for writing. Your impact stuck. I still carry it with me.

To Angela Morrison at Wiley. Thank you for your support, guidance, and patience. This book is infinitely stronger because of you.

And to every brilliant human who let me interview them and trusted me to tell part of their story: Tobi Oluwole, Morgan J. Ingram, Linda Le, April Little, Elfried Samba, Aleah Roseen, and Sharayah Wilson. You made this book real. Your stories made the pages breathe. Thank you for sharing your time, your wisdom, and your words.

Introduction

The first time I *really* felt out of place, like an outsider, was in the sixth grade. I was sitting in the cafeteria, talking to my friends when one of them looked at me and said, "You talk so white!"

It wasn't the first time I'd felt different (believe me, I'd already had more than enough awkward moments to last a lifetime), but this one stuck. It was a declaration, not a question or an observation. There was judgment in her tone, like I was doing something wrong, but there was also an undertone of pride. Like this was a compliment, something I should be thankful for. Everyone laughed and moved on, but I felt her words settle deep in my chest, sparking a faint but unmistakable question: *Am I different? And if so ... is that bad?*

I spent the majority of my childhood in Carmel, Indiana, where being "different" wasn't exactly celebrated. It was a polished, wealthy suburb where the neighborhoods looked like movie sets, lawns were manicured to Stepford-level perfection, and I was often the only Black girl in the room. Sometimes the only Black person, period.

My mom, who immigrated to Brooklyn from Jamaica as a child, always found a way to joke about it. "Our family doubled the Black population in Carmel," she'd say with a laugh. And while I'd laugh too, it also hit on a deeper truth I had to face as I grew up: I was constantly navigating spaces where I wasn't really *seen*.

That feeling didn't disappear when I entered corporate America. It just changed shape and evolved. In my first corporate job, I was often the only person of color in the room. The only first-generation American. The only woman. I got used to the sound of my own voice echoing in rooms that didn't look or think like me.

And it wasn't just about being different. It felt like my every move was being scrutinized. I'd often feel like I was being asked to represent the entire Black community (and all marginalized communities, for that matter). There was this sense that every word I said, every decision I made, was being interpreted through a filter I didn't install. I often felt like I wasn't just carrying the weight of my own job or success. I was representing something bigger. Something "other." So, I tried to fit. I softened my voice. Smoothed my edges. Hid my tattoos. Mastered the art of code-switching so well, I could've put it on my résumé. I even tried to change the way I *laughed*. But no matter how hard I worked to belong, I never felt like I did.

Eventually, I hit a breaking point, as so many of us do. That moment when you realize that no amount of adapting would make you feel at home in a system that was never designed for you. And if you're going to do all this work, it might as well be in service of building something that fits *you*.

This book started with a question about belonging—how to find your place in spaces that weren't built with you in mind. But it didn't stay there. As I wrote, that question kept evolving. What happens when you're done twisting yourself into a thousand different shapes to make other people comfortable? What happens once you've claimed your space?

So, yes, this book is about imposter syndrome, identity, code-switching, and all the subtle ways we shrink ourselves to survive in rooms that feel unfamiliar. But it's also about what happens *after* that:

- *After* you stop trying to prove yourself
- *After* you decide to take up space

- *After* you realize you get to decide what your career looks like and what your life feels like

When you decide to build something of your own, this book is about that build.

It's about crafting a career that reflects who you are, how you work best, and what actually matters to you. It's about learning to treat your time, energy, and skills like the finite, valuable resources they are—and making choices accordingly. It's about ditching the myth that you have to follow one linear path to be successful and instead creating a rhythm that's flexible, profitable, energizing, and *yours.*

For me, that looked like this:

- Pivoting out of film and into marketing
- Launching a business
- Letting go of full-time roles that didn't fit
- Reclaiming time for writing and side hustles
- Walking away from offers that looked great on paper but came with a hefty side of burnout
- Reimagining what work could feel like, and building a career that flexed with my life, not against it

And that's what you'll find in this book: stories, frameworks, and prompts to help you carve out your version of success, build the systems to sustain it, and understand your own rhythm well enough to stop outsourcing your self-worth to someone's milestones.

This book is for you if:

- You've ever walked into a room and felt like you didn't belong, like you had to shrink yourself or smooth out your edges just to be taken seriously.

- You've felt the weight of imposter syndrome, the kind that whispers you're not good enough or that you're just faking it, no matter how hard you work or how much you achieve.
- You've wondered how to balance ambition with authenticity, to build a career or a life that doesn't force you to choose between success and staying true to yourself.
- You're tired of measuring success by someone else's rules and want to build a career that actually reflects your goals, values, and capacity.
- You're carving your own path and want to make it sustainable without losing yourself in the process.

And honestly, this book is for me too:

- For 12-year-old Brianna, who wasn't sure whether "different" was a compliment or a warning.
- For the early-career me who didn't know how to take up space without apology.
- And for the woman I am now, who's still learning how to lead, rest, pivot, and build in ways that feel honest.

We're not here by accident. We're here because we're qualified. Because we've done the work. And because we're ready to build something better, on our terms.

Let's get to work.

Chapter 1

Understanding Imposter Syndrome

Have you ever walked into a room and instantly questioned if you belonged there? Maybe it was a meeting where every face turned toward you, expecting you to prove your worth. Or perhaps you walked into a room and thought, *I'm not qualified to be here.*

Let me be the first to tell you that you're *definitely* not alone. That feeling (the tightening in your chest, the mental rehearsing of your credentials, the instinct to shrink or overcompensate) is a common experience for many of us who occupy identities that aren't the default. Many of us have our own version of the "I don't belong here" narrative.

It's exhausting, isn't it? But it doesn't have to define you.

For years, I struggled with this too. I used to believe that I had to wait for someone to invite me in, give me a seat at the table, or grant me permission to belong. But I eventually realized that the table *exists* because of people like us: people who bring unique perspectives, lived experiences, and new, fresh ideas that challenge the status quo.

Imposter syndrome, at its core, is that nagging voice that makes us question our worth and whether we deserve our place in the room. But let me tell you, you *do* belong. And you don't have to wait for someone else to validate that for you.

What Is Imposter Syndrome?

You've probably heard the term before, but what does *imposter syndrome* actually mean?

Simply put, the National Library of Medicine defines imposter syndrome as "self-doubt of intellect, skills, or accomplishments among high-achieving individuals."[1] It could sound like this:

- *I don't belong.*

- *I'm not qualified.*

- *Despite all the hard work I've put in and all of my wins, I'm just pretending to know what I'm doing. It doesn't matter how many wins I rack up or how many people sing my praises. I'm a fraud.*

And trust me, it's not just a catchy phrase thrown around LinkedIn and Instagram posts. It's very real.

That internal battle can show up anywhere, but it's especially common in environments where you're the "only one" in the room: the only Black woman, the only person of color, the only first-generation American, the only one who doesn't come from a traditional background. And this self-doubt can feel amplified by systemic inequities.

According to *The State of Black Women in Corporate America*, a report released by Lean In in 2020, for every 100 men promoted to manager, only 58 Black women are promoted (despite the fact that Black women ask for promotions at the same rate as men). And for every 100 men hired into managerial roles, only 64 Black women are hired.[2]

Between racial bias, microaggressions, and the wage gap, the corporate world isn't exactly a level playing field. And that reality can create an external pressure that manifests as (you guessed it) imposter syndrome. Maybe it's not that we always *feel* unqualified. Perhaps, for some of us, our qualifications are questioned and minimized at every turn.

Reflections for You

Before we go deeper, I want to pause and give you a moment to reflect. Think about a time when you felt like an outsider in a personal or professional setting.

- What triggered that feeling? Was it something external or internal?
- How did you respond in the moment? Did you shrink, adapt, or stand firm?
- In hindsight, what would you have done differently?

These moments don't define us, but they can teach us something about how we will show up in spaces where belonging feels elusive. Write your reflections down. They'll serve as a map for navigating future challenges.

The Psychological Impact of Imposter Syndrome

According to research by Dr. Pauline Clancy and Dr. Suzanne Ames, who coined the term *imposter phenomenon*, imposter syndrome can be linked to higher levels of anxiety, depression, burnout, and self-sabotage. When you feel like you must fake it, that can lead to burnout. You keep pushing yourself harder than necessary, working to prove something (to yourself, to others) that doesn't need proving. The damage isn't just professional. It's psychological.

And that's where it can get even trickier. Raise your hand if you've ever caught yourself overcompensating because you're experiencing imposter syndrome. Maybe you overwork, obsess over every minute detail, or simply refuse to delegate tasks and projects because you don't trust anyone else's judgment. When something doesn't lead to the perfection that you expect, the cycle of self-doubt intensifies and resets. You become trapped in an exhausting, unproductive loop.

It's not just about not being *given* opportunities you deserve. It's about the constant feeling of being "on guard," of never knowing if your success is actually being tolerated or seen as a threat. This level of scrutiny forces many of us into a position of feeling like imposters, even when we have more than earned our place. And it's not always about fixing ourselves. It's also about recognizing and challenging the systems that contribute to these feelings.

Systemic Roots of Imposter Syndrome (It's Not Just in Your Head)

April Little, an executive career coach, says it best: "Imposter syndrome isn't something inherent or innate. It's more often imposed upon us by our environment and internalized over time."

For marginalized communities, imposter syndrome often stems from workplaces that

- dismiss or overshadow our voices,
- fail to recognize diverse perspectives, or
- perpetuate systems of exclusion.

April refers to this as the planting of "seeds of discord" in these environments. "I don't believe people enter the workplace inherently feeling like frauds. These feelings develop when their expertise is dismissed, their voices are overshadowed, or their approach is labeled as 'wrong.'"[3]

We have to stop pretending that imposter syndrome is just a buzzword about personal insecurity. Can it manifest that way? Absolutely.

But for marginalized communities, it's often a direct response to an environment that constantly undermines our worth because the systems, spaces, and environments we navigate aren't neutral.

A Personal Reckoning with Imposter Syndrome

Let me take you to a recent moment: a VIP networking dinner where I was the only Black woman at the table (actually, the only woman, period). Picture this: White male CEOs, CMOs, and CROs who've been at the top of their fields for decades. I was honored to be there, but in the back of my head, that voice started whispering:

- *Maybe I'm not supposed to be here.*
- *Maybe they regret inviting me.*
- *What if I embarrass myself?*

I could feel myself slipping into a smaller version of me. It didn't matter that I'd spent more than 13 years building my career, that I was a keynote speaker, or that I was a published writer. In that moment, I felt like 21-year-old me: freshly graduated, unsure, and trying to prove I deserved a seat at the table.

It's funny, right, how we can become so absorbed by our own insecurities and perceived shortcomings that we forget everything else? The fight against imposter syndrome is a personal one, but it's also universal. It's the quiet work we do to remind ourselves that we are more than the doubts in our head (and others' preconceived notions about us).

Here's what I wish I'd told myself that night, and what I'm telling you now: Your presence in these spaces isn't an accident, a favor, or a fluke. You've earned it. You belong there. And when imposter syndrome rears its ugly head, there are ways to fight back.

Reframing Imposter Syndrome: Tools to Shift Your Mindset

This feeling about "belonging" is about more than just being in the room. It's about feeling confident and grounded in your place there. But when imposter syndrome creeps in, it can be hard to hold onto that sense of belonging. The good news: you can actively reframe those feelings and shift your mindset with a few key tools. Let's break them down.

Recognize and Name the Doubt

One of the first steps to reframing imposter syndrome is identifying the feeling when it arises. That inner voice whispering, *You're not good enough,* thrives in ambiguity and in silence. The moment you name it, you begin to take away some of its power.

Here's how it works:

- Every time you walk into a room where you feel out of place, remind yourself: *I am here for a reason.* Write it on a sticky note. Repeat it in your head like a mantra. That internal shift is the first step toward owning your space.

- When the thought *I'm not qualified to be here* pops up, pause and say to yourself (or even out loud), "This is imposter syndrome talking."

- Give it a name. Maybe it's "Self-Doubt Shayla" or "Negative Nancy." It sounds silly, I know, but naming the thought creates distance between you and the feeling. It becomes something you can address instead of something that defines you.

Think about this the next time you're preparing for a big presentation or interviewing for a job. When the thought pops into your head—*What if they realize I'm not actually good at this?*—stop yourself right there and say, "No. This is just imposter syndrome showing up again." Then follow it up with evidence from your Brag Book (covered next) to remind yourself why you're qualified.

Naming the doubt is about acknowledging your feelings so they don't control you. It's not about dismissing them.

Create a Brag Book

When self-doubt strikes, having concrete, historical evidence of your accomplishments can make all the difference. That's where your Brag Book comes in. Think of it as your personal highlight reel: a collection of wins, big or small, that you can turn to when imposter syndrome starts whispering lies again.

Here's what you can include:

- Positive feedback from managers, colleagues, or clients/customers.
- Metrics that showcase your impact.
- Screenshots of testimonials, compliments, or encouraging messages.
- Notes about projects you're proud of and why they mattered.

Don't let yourself skip over accolades. Let yourself soak in those wins. When you're reminded of your value, it becomes harder to believe the story that you don't belong in the room or at the table.

Ask Yourself Better Questions

Instead of spiraling into asking yourself *What if I'm not good enough?*, try shifting your questions, like in Table 1.1.

Table 1.1 Asking Better Questions

Original Statement	Reframe
What if I'm not good enough?	What strengths can I lean into here?
When will they realize that I shouldn't be here?	How can I add value in this situation?
I'm nowhere near as impressive as the other people in this room.	I'm grateful to bring [this skill set], [this perspective], and [this talent] to the table.
I'm not qualified to be here.	What has prepared me for this moment/role/opportunity?

Find Your Anchor

When you step into a room where you feel like you don't belong or haven't earned your spot, what keeps you grounded? What reminds you that you deserve to be there? This is your anchor—the thing that holds you steady when doubt tries to pull you off course.

You can lean into your anchor:

- *Your preparation.* The work you've put in to get to this moment or the homework you've done to remind yourself that you're ready.

- *Your values.* Remember what you stand for and how your presence aligns with your goals, mission, and path.

- *Past wins.* Look back at your Brag Book! Think of a moment when you doubted yourself but still showed up and succeeded.

For me, it's preparation. I remind myself that I've done the work and I'm here because I've earned my spot. Find what keeps you steady and hold onto it.

Find Your Mirrors and Windows

Surround yourself with mentors and peers who reflect your experiences and can relate to your journey ("mirrors") and those who offer perspectives different from yours ("windows"). It's about building your confidence but also about broadening your lens.

While *mentors* and *sponsors* are sometimes used interchangeably, they play different roles in your career growth. Mentors are those who guide you. They offer advice, help you develop your skills, and support your journey. They typically help you navigate challenges and offer a sounding board and safe space for growth.

Sponsors, on the other hand, play a more strategic role in your career advancement. Unlike mentors, sponsors *actively* advocate for you in a room that you may not be in. They vouch for your skills, recommend you for projects and opportunities, and openly believe in your potential. Sometimes this means putting their own reputation on the line to help elevate you, which can be crucial for breaking through systemic barriers and gaining visibility.

Seeking out these relationships, investing in them, and doing the same for others won't just help you. These relationships create a network of advocacy, centered around amplifying everyone's voices and accomplishments, instead of amplifying only those who speak the loudest.

Take Up Space (Literally and Figuratively)

When you feel small, make a conscious effort to take up space. Sit up straight, make eye contact (if possible), and resist the urge to apologize for existing, asking a question, or sharing your opinion.

Our body language can reinforce our internal confidence. Remember, you belong here just as much as anyone else.

On the flip side, here's what not to do:

- *Don't shrink yourself physically.* Slouching, crossing your arms tightly, or leaning away from the table or group can make you appear uncertain, even if you don't feel that way deep down.

- *Don't preface your ideas with disclaimers.* Two phrases I frequently hear during calls: "This might be a stupid question, but …" and "I'm not sure if this is right, but …" These can unintentionally diminish your credibility, even unintentionally. Your thoughts are valid. Present them with confidence.

- *Don't wait for permission to contribute.* Whether it's waiting for someone to explicitly ask for your input or feeling hesitant to speak up in meetings, know that your perspective matters. Step into the conversation with intention.

Reflections for You

Now it's your turn:

- Think back to a time when you felt inferior to the people around you or like an outsider in the room. What did you tell yourself in that moment? What could you have told yourself instead?

- What's one part of your story that makes you stand out? How can you embrace that as one of your strengths?

- Who are the people you can lean on for support when self-doubt takes over?

These aren't just rhetorical questions. Take the time to write them down, sit with them, and let your answers guide you.

Is insecurity real? Yes. Can we feel uncomfortable and unqualified for reasons other than systemic exclusion? Absolutely. But instead of internalizing the doubt we so commonly feel in corporate settings, maybe we need to start to externalize them and recognize that many of these doubts are part of a system that hasn't been designed for us to succeed. We need to give ourselves permission to stop blaming our minds and shortcomings and start challenging the environment.

But self-advocacy doesn't mean you'll become immune to self-doubt. It also doesn't mean that we think we're flawless, can abandon a growth mindset, or refuse to find areas for improvement in our own careers and work ethic.

It means acknowledging that many of these feelings are often a reflection of the world we live in, not reflections of our inherent inadequacies or shortcomings. When we commit to reframing these feelings as natural responses to unnatural systems, instead of *always* labeling them as signals that we need to "fix" ourselves, we take the first step toward empowering ourselves to take action.

Takeaways

- Imposter syndrome isn't just a "me" problem. The key is acknowledging it and learning how to shift your mindset to work through it.
- Your worth doesn't need to be validated by others. Recognizing and trusting your own abilities is a major step in shutting down feelings of inferiority and of not belonging.
- There are many tools that can help you shift your mindset; use them!

Chapter 2

Acknowledging Your Worth and Owning Your Impact

Let's start with a simple truth: You are worthy. Yes, you. Just as you are, with *all* of your passions, talents, and experiences.

It's so easy to lose sight of this, especially in a world that has a way of placing us in a constant state of comparison. Between social media, less-than-ideal work environments, and the way others humble brag (or even lie) about their own successes, we are led to feel small, unaccomplished, or (worst of all) like an imposter. But acknowledging our worth is about being real with ourselves about the value we bring to the table.

Your journey matters, however "messy," winding, or unconventional it may seem. The impact you've made at work, in your relationships, and in your community is all worth acknowledging and celebrating.

Recognize the Need to Acknowledge Your Work and Worth

Let's pause and take a moment. Think about your closest friend, family member, or loved one. Someone you *genuinely* admire. Picture them in your mind. Now list (mentally or on paper) all the ways this person is amazing. Maybe they're ridiculously good at making people laugh, or they always come through with the best advice *right* when you need it. Maybe they've built an incredible career, or they have a knack for bringing people out of their shell and making people feel comfortable and welcomed. Let your brain wander and collect some of the reasons.

Now imagine you hear this same incredible human minimizing all those accomplishments and traits you love them for. Picture them saying, "Oh, I'm not that good," while they wave you off, or "My success is just luck, really." Or even worse, "I haven't done anything special." How does that feel, witnessing them dismiss everything you see as *undeniably valuable* about them? A little infuriating, right?

If I overheard my best friend or my mom talking about themselves like that, I'd want to shake them and say, "Stop! Are you kidding? You're so talented, insightful, and capable. *You're amazing.*"

Well, unfortunately, you've probably done the same thing to yourself. I'd bet good money that you've downplayed your achievements, brushed off the compliments, or even told yourself *all* the reasons why your hard work, your perspective, your wins don't really matter. It's a bit hypocritical, isn't it? We'd be the first to leap to our best friend's defense, but when it comes to ourselves, we let imposter syndrome and self-criticism have a field day.

The Danger of Downplaying Yourself

Here's the deal. Downplaying your accomplishments, or refusing to acknowledge your impact, isn't harmless. It chips away at your confidence, sabotages your growth, and creates a fog of false modesty that makes it harder for others to see and understand your impact and value. If you're not clear about your own value and what you bring to the table, how can you expect other people to be? When we diminish our accomplishments, we give others the power to control the narrative about our work.

April Little calls this the "Invisible Contributor" trap. She explains, "[These women] work diligently and actively avoid being seen. They believe their work should speak for itself, which is a massive mistake. This habit leads to others speaking for them and sometimes even taking credit for their contributions."[1]

Sound familiar?

Imagine you've spent weeks preparing a detailed report for a big meeting. When the day comes, you let your coworker present it, thinking, *It's fine. My work will speak for itself.* But when it doesn't, and when your name isn't mentioned, who gets the credit? Your coworker. This is what happens when we hand over the reins of our narrative to someone else.

See Your Value for What It Is

If the idea of self-advocacy (or self-promotion) feels intimidating, let's start small. Grab a notebook and reflect on these:

- What's one success or project you're proud of that you've never talked about?

- How would you describe this accomplishment to a mentor or friend who genuinely wants to celebrate you?

- If you heard someone else downplaying a similar win, what would you say to them?

The goal for these prompts is to start to rewire how you see your own contributions. The next time that voice in your head tells you *It wasn't a big deal*, come back to what you've written.

Then tackle a few of the excuses you might catch yourself using by reframing them; refer to Table 2.1.

Table 2.1 Reframing Excuses

Excuse	Reframe
"I don't want to come across as arrogant."	Sharing your truth isn't the same as being arrogant. It's clarity. Communicating your value helps others understand your impact, and that's essential for growth.
"My team/CEO/manager already knows the work I've done (and the impact I have)."	Don't assume they do. People are busy and focused on their own work. Take the lead in making your impact clear.
"It's not that big of a deal."	If someone else did the same thing, would you see it as a small deal? Or would you be impressed?

For many of us, downplaying our worth feels almost instinctive. But owning your contributions sets a precedent not just for you but also for others who need to see what's possible.

Recognize That Your Unconventional Journey Can Be Your Greatest Strength

I didn't have the most conventional entry into marketing. I studied film and media studies in college and planned to move to New Zealand and work as a screenwriter. But life had other plans. I pivoted to marketing, a field I'd never even considered before college. At first, I questioned whether my background had value. Surrounded by business grads and MBAs, I felt out of place.

What I didn't see then was that my unconventional path gave me a unique perspective. For example, years of studying film and writing screenplays taught me to understand pacing, tone, and how to keep an audience engaged. Those hours spent dissecting films taught me how to understand the psychology of storytelling, communication, and what resonates emotionally, all of which are skills that translate perfectly to understanding consumer behavior. It all starts with reframing your narrative.

Reframe Your Narrative and Reflect on Your Strengths

Instead of viewing your nontraditional background as a "weakness," ask yourself, "How does it give me a fresh lens that others might not have?" Write down one unique skill or perspective from your past experience and connect it to your current role or project. Ask yourself:

- What is a skill I've mastered in a job or project that initially felt unrelated to my career goals?
- How can that skill give me a unique edge in my field today?
- What insights or experiences do I bring to the table that my peers might lack?

Own Your Journey in Conversations

When someone questions your career journey (or when you find *yourself* questioning it), reframing your story is essential. If you feel the need to defend your choices, try to see this as an opportunity to highlight the strengths you bring to the table. Use the prompts in Table 2.2 as inspiration for real-life situations.

Table 2.2 Reframing Prompts

Situation	What Not to Say	How to Reframe It
Networking event	"Oh, my background is all over the place."	"I started in [X], where I learned to [Y]. That foundation led me to [Z] now."
Job interview	"I don't have a traditional background, but I'll do my best to learn." "I know I don't have the same training as others, but I'll figure it out."	"My background has given me a fresh perspective on [X], [Y], and Z."
Explaining career breaks and/or pivots	"I took a break because I didn't know what I wanted to do."	"I used my time off to explore new skills and passions, which ultimately led me to [current field/role]."

> ### Key Reflection
> Your nontraditional path is your strength. It's not a limitation. The skills, insights, and experiences you've gained along the way equip you in ways you might not even recognize yet. Own them.

Steps to Overcoming Self-doubt

Now that you understand how important it is to recognize your self-worth and to minimize your feelings of insecurity, you can take affirmative steps to overcome your negative feelings and any sense of imposter syndrome (as described in Chapter 1).

Name It to Tame It

The first step in overcoming imposter syndrome is recognizing and labeling the feeling when it shows up. Imposter syndrome thrives in isolation, feeding on the belief that you're the only one who feels this way. But trust me—you're not alone. Any of the people you admire, from CEOs to creatives to your favorite celebrity, have dealt with the same doubts. It's all about learning how to confront and manage these feelings instead of letting them dictate our lives.

Identify the Feeling

Sometimes, imposter syndrome doesn't show up as a loud, obvious thought. It can manifest subtly:

- *Procrastination.* You avoid starting a project because you're scared of not being "good enough."
- *Overpreparation.* You spend hours on something that should've taken 30 minutes, hoping to compensate for your "lack of expertise."
- *Downplaying your accomplishments.* When someone praises your work, you say, "Oh, it was nothing!" or "I just got lucky."

If you notice these patterns, pause. Instead of letting them continue to spiral, take a moment to name what's happening. Say to yourself (or even out loud), "This is imposter syndrome talking."

Acknowledge and Share the Feeling

Start by reflecting on your experiences with imposter syndrome:

- When was the last time you felt like an imposter?
- What triggered it? Was it a new role, a challenging project, or walking into a room full of people you didn't know?
- How did you respond in that moment? Did you shrink, overcompensate, or avoid altogether? Or did you tackle the feeling head-on?

Once you've identified the feeling, think about sharing it with someone you trust. You might say:

- "I've been feeling a little out of my depth lately, and it's making me question my abilities."
- "I think I've been struggling with imposter syndrome, and I'd love to hear if you've experienced this too."

Opening up can feel vulnerable, but it's also incredibly liberating. A shared connection can be a powerful reminder that you're not alone and that imposter syndrome is a feeling, not a fact.

Keep Documenting the Feeling

Each time you feel imposter syndrome creeping in, jot down the following:

- The situation or trigger.
- What the voice in your head is saying.
- A counterargument or evidence that disproves this doubt.

Consider this example:

- *Trigger:* Giving a presentation at work.
- *Thought:* "I don't know what I'm talking about. Someone else would've done this better."
- *Counterargument:* "I've spent weeks preparing for this. I know this material better than anyone else in the room."

By documenting these patterns, you can start to see them and build a toolkit of responses to push back against self-doubt.

Put Your Doubts on Trial

April Little has a brilliant method for tackling imposter syndrome: cross-examine your doubts like a lawyer. Ask yourself:

- Is this a formal requirement for my role?
- Have I done this successfully before?
- Have I received feedback to support this doubt?

By the end, most of your doubts won't have a leg to stand on, and they end up crumbling under scrutiny.

Here's an example: You're stepping into a new leadership role and doubt your ability to guide a team. Ask yourself:

- *Requirement:* Does leadership require me to have all the answers upfront? (No, it requires delegation, decision-making skills, and deep expertise in your space.)
- *Past Success:* Have I successfully led projects or mentored others before? (Yes.)
- *Feedback:* Have others recognized my leadership potential? (Yes, my previous manager specifically encouraged me to apply for this role.)

When you approach doubts with evidence, you can unravel false narratives. And when a doubt does hold water (for example, a real skill gap), treat this as an opportunity to learn and grow.

Own Your Achievements

Many of us (myself included) were raised to value humility. It was ingrained as a virtue, and there's nothing inherently wrong with that! But there's a huge difference between bragging and clearly communicating your impact. You're not shouting from the rooftops just to hear yourself speak; you're making sure your voice is heard in the room.

Practice owning your wins. Start with small achievements and then work your way up, or if it's easier, start with the big achievements and work your way down.

Practice "I'm Proud" Statements

Like I said, you can start small. Get comfortable saying these phrases to yourself and to others:

"I'm Proud"	Example
"I'm proud ..."	"... of how I navigated that challenging project."
"My contributions ..."	"... helped the team hit our goal."
"I led ..."	"... that project to a successful launch."

Build Your Personal Board of Directors

You've probably heard that you're the sum of the five people you spend the most time with. I'm not sure if I fully believe in that math, but I will say this: Who you surround yourself with matters. A lot.

In a world where it's easy to feel misunderstood or undervalued, your "personal board of directors" can be the compass that keeps you headed in the right direction.

Think of it like having your own mini-committee dedicated to championing your growth and worth. This could mean finding a mentor, a business coach, or just a group of like-minded colleagues and individuals. The bottom line is, having a network is critical.

Look for Alignment, Not Just Experience

It's tempting to want a mentor who has "done it all," is super high up in their field, or rakes in serious cash. But alignment in values and goals is a lot more important than your mentor's spot on the Fortune 500. You want someone who doesn't just see your potential achievements but also sees *you*, period. That means someone who respects what you stand for and how you like to work and who doesn't dismiss your passions. That's the person who will give feedback that resonates (not just feedback that looks good on paper).

Seek Out Community

Beyond one-on-one mentorship, a group dynamic can keep you accountable, encourage you, and might even make you a little competitive (in a good way!). Whether from a mastermind group, a professional network, or a Slack channel, find the people who are in the thick of growth and discovery, like you. A room (real or virtual) where everyone is celebrating each other's wins and sharing each other's struggles can be powerful.

Don't underestimate the magic that happens when a community of like-minded humans decides to lift each other up. When you have that kind of steady support, you'll see others stepping into their worth and cheering you on when you do the same.

Speak Your Impact into Existence

Once you've done the work of acknowledging your worth and impact internally, it's time to let the world in on the secret. Internal confidence is beautiful and crucial, but if it never leaves the confines of your own mind, it can only go so far, right?

I used to believe that speaking my impact into existence meant I was arrogant or trying to hog the spotlight. But what it really is, is articulating why your work matters and how can it benefit those around you.

Tips for Communicating Your Impact

- Frame your impact around value and lead with the "why." People perk up when they hear you articulate the value you deliver, not just the tasks.

- Inject your personality! Fortunately, gone are the days where we need to be robotic or formulaic.

- Back it up with results or stories. You don't need a laundry list of stats, but a brief anecdote or example tells people you're not just talk. Real outcomes resonate.

Remember: Owning your impact makes you *clear,* not arrogant— clear about what you offer, why it matters, and how people can benefit from working alongside you. If you find yourself hesitating to speak up, think back to your personal board of directors or your community. They already see your value. Why not let others see it too?

Instead of working in silence, hoping people "get it," you have the opportunity to actively shape how the world perceives your contributions. You can weave your personal story and voice into everything you do. That's when your career stops feeling like an endless, or directionless, grind and starts feeling like a platform for genuine impact and influence.

Takeaways

- Acknowledge your worth regularly and practice speaking about your impact with confidence.
- Quiet the voice of imposter syndrome by confronting the thoughts that tell you you're not quite good enough. Instead, embrace growth and learning along the way.
- Following the steps to overcoming self-doubt will lead you far along the path to a career that is meaningful and fulfilling.

Chapter 3

Identifying and Embracing Your Strengths

So many of us spend so much time obsessing over our weaknesses—the things that we're "just not good at," or what we perceive to be missing in ourselves. In a world where hustle culture is celebrated and people are constantly told how to "be better" and "do more, more, more," it's easy to overlook how much power and potential we have within us right now. And it's even easier to feel like we're constantly behind, focusing on improvement at the expense of self-appreciation.

But what if I told you the power to move forward already exists within you, hidden in your strengths?

These strengths include the technical skills you've acquired and the tasks you've mastered at work, but they're also the unique traits, approaches, and perspectives you bring to the table. They are what set you apart, and fully leaning into them can become the foundation for a fulfilling and successful career, a career that is uniquely *you*.

Recognize the Strengths You Already Possess

One of my early managers, Don, once told me, "You're great at breaking down complex ideas and making them digestible." At the time, I shrugged it off, thinking, *Isn't that just part of my job?*

But as I started paying attention, I realized that simplifying and storytelling were both recurring patterns in my work. From distilling dense data into actionable campaigns to explaining marketing and data to clients in relatable ways, this was something I naturally gravitated toward. And it's turned out to be one of my most valuable professional assets. Now it's your turn to identify some of yours.

Let's start by doing a quick inventory of your strengths. Write down at least five strengths that stand out to you, based on your own reflections or feedback you've received from others.

Ask yourself these questions:

- What skills did I use to excel in this situation?
- What feedback have I received from others that highlights my strengths?
- What tasks or projects come naturally to me, even when they're a bit challenging?

Don't limit yourself to just technical skills (design, video editing, etc.). Include interpersonal skills, personality traits, and approaches to your work that make you effective (communication, empathy, etc.). No strength is too "small" to acknowledge.

Take a step back from the technical requirements of your work. Think about what it is that you love to do:

- What part of your work do you "lose yourself" in?
- What comes naturally to you?
- What questions do you enjoy solving?

The answers may not always fit the mold, but they'll help guide you to a deeper understanding of your own skill set.

Go Beyond Your Résumé

Many of us treat our strengths and skill sets like a LinkedIn profile or a section on our résumé: just checklists of certifications, job titles, or hard skills. For me, it would look something like:

- ✔ Field: Influencer marketing

- ✔ Field: Growth marketing

- ✔ Certifications: HubSpot and Google Analytics

- ✔ Tech: Adobe Creative Suite

Check, check, check. You get the picture, and I'm sure you could list many of your own. But many of your strengths run much deeper than a box you can tick off. They're about who you *are* when you show up to work (or to any space, really), not just what you've learned. Think of them as the heartbeat of your professional, and personal, identity.

Sure, you can print your technical skills on a résumé, but what about your ability to stay calm in a crisis? Or how great you are at taking a really complex and obscure problem, breaking it down into manageable, digestible pieces, then tackling it efficiently and effectively? These are strengths too. They're the intangible threads that tie together *what* you do and *how* you do it. And they're often the true differentiators that clients, employers, and teams remember you for, long after they've forgotten which Adobe certifications you have.

Uncover Your "Quiet" Strengths

Think of your "quiet" strengths as the intangibles, the attributes that don't always show up in a formal skill set but are invaluable to your work and relationships. Your quiet strengths are woven into how you approach collaboration, conflict resolution, and even self-care. And when you recognize that these traits carry as much weight as the bullet points in your LinkedIn profile, you open the door to leveraging them in meaningful ways. The first step is to uncover them.

Think about your day-to-day work and interactions. Ask yourself:

- What's something I do regularly that feels small to me but makes a big impact on others?

- When was the last time someone thanked or acknowledged me for something that felt like second nature to me?

- What are some recent moments when I felt *truly alive* in my work? (That rush of energy can indicate a quiet or core strength at play.)

Tie Your Quiet Strengths Back to the Bigger Picture

The key to leveraging your strengths and skills is recognizing how they align with your personal and professional goals. For example, let's say one of your skills is staying calm under pressure. Think about how that can help you lead challenging projects or navigate high-stakes conversations with clients or company leaders.

Of course, you still need the technical know-how, and that shouldn't be discounted. These quieter strengths are often what leave lasting impressions on people and differentiate you in competitive environments.

Leverage Your Strengths to Create Opportunities for Yourself

Recognizing your strengths is only half the battle. It's what you do with them that counts. Your strengths, once identified *and* embraced, are like a compass, guiding and pointing you toward opportunities that align with your unique skill set and abilities. But opportunities don't always come knocking (unfortunately). Sometimes we must build the door ourselves.

So, how can you take your strengths and use them as tools to create tangible, fulfilling opportunities for growth, impact, and success? It starts with finding alignment where your strengths, interests, and opportunities intersect.

Find Alignment in Your Work: The Three-Question Framework

Let's start by uncovering where your strengths align with opportunities. This is about understanding not just what you're good at but also what brings you joy and where you naturally shine. To do this, ask yourself three questions:

1. **What am I great at? What am I good at?**
   - *Great at:* These are your standout talents, the things that come effortlessly to you and consistently deliver top-tier results. You might overlook them because they feel second nature, but trust me, they are your secret weapons. These are often your strongest assets.
   - *Good at:* These are areas where you're competent but not necessarily the best. They're still strengths, but there's room to refine and grow.

2. What do I enjoy doing?

Not all strengths are enjoyable, and not all enjoyable tasks align with your goals or career path. This question can help you identify where your passions intersect with your abilities. Ask yourself:

- Which tasks or projects make me feel energized?
- What do I look forward to in my workday?

3. What feels easy for me?

More often than not, your natural strengths are hidden in what feels effortless. These are the things you can do without over-thinking, even when others find them challenging. I once had a coworker, Emily, who was a natural project manager. She had an incredible ability to corral teams, manage our boss's expectations, and set realistic timelines. She kept everyone in check, from our marketing team to the CEO. It was a sight to behold.

But don't discount difficult work you enjoy. It's equally valuable.

> ### Exercise
>
> Write down three to five things that come easily to you. Think about the times when people have asked some variation of, "How do you do that so effortlessly?"

Connect the Dots: The Overlap of Strengths, Joy, and Ease

Once you've answered the three questions, take a step back and look for patterns and overlaps:

- Where do your strengths, enjoyment, and ease intersect?
- What are the common threads in your answers?

This intersection is where your highest-value strengths lie. These are the areas where you're most likely to thrive, feel fulfilled, and create meaningful opportunities. So what do we do with this information?

Build Your Opportunity Roadmap

Now that we've identified your core strengths and quiet strengths, it's time to turn them into actionable opportunities. Let's translate your self-awareness into tangible steps:

1. *Write down your strengths.* Choose three strengths you identified in the previous exercise.

2. *Brainstorm aligned opportunities.* For each strength, brainstorm at least one concrete opportunity where you can leverage it. Think about roles, side hustles, or projects that align with your abilities.

3. *Incorporate your quiet strengths.* Take note of where your quiet strengths can fit in with each opportunity. How can you leverage those unique skills and abilities?

4. *Create an action plan.* Write down one actionable next step for each opportunity. Be specific and make it something you can start today or next week.

Example Roadmaps

- *Strength:* Strong public speaking skills.
- *Opportunity:* Apply to speak at a local conference.
- *Action Plan:* Research upcoming events, draft a topic proposal, and submit an application.
- *Strength:* Natural problem-solving ability.
- *Opportunity:* Lead a process improvement project at work for increased visibility within your team and company.
- *Action Plan:* Identify inefficiencies in any current workflows, outline proposed solutions, and present them to your manager.

By actively creating opportunities for yourself, you don't have to wait for someone else to lead the way. You can take charge of your own career.

Bring It Full Circle: Reflect and Refine

After implementing your roadmap, make sure you take time to reflect:

- Did this opportunity align with my strengths and passions?
- Did I feel energized or drained by the process?
- What adjustments can I make to ensure the next opportunity is even more aligned?

Remember, leveraging your strengths is an ongoing practice. As you grow and evolve, so will your opportunities. Stay curious, adaptable, and intentional as you apply your talents and skill set. It's important to remember that you don't have to wait for the right door to open. You can build it yourself. And when you do, you'll find that the opportunities on the other side are not just rewarding but are deeply aligned with who you are and what you bring to the table.

Celebrate Your Unique Strengths Without Comparison

Years ago, early in my career, I worked as a photographer for the Arizona Diamondbacks at Chase Field. As a rookie, I was terrified and surrounded by pros who'd been shooting photos for years. Their shots were the kind that went viral on ESPN (literally). What was I even doing there?

One afternoon, during a quiet, low-stakes game, I was crouched in the photographers' section, flipping through my shots. Nearby, a seasoned photographer was talking about a time-lapse sequence he'd nailed of a pitcher's wind-up. I glanced at his camera, and the familiar wave of doubt washed over me: *Ugh. I'll never get a shot that good.*

I decided right then and there to find my own winning shot of the day. And out of the corner of my eye, I noticed the afternoon sun shining on Jake Lamb, one of the infielders. I slipped out of the dugout, climbed into the stands, and found a vantage point where

I could see him clearly. That's when I captured one of my favorite shots of the season: a beam of sunlight cutting across the field, illuminating Lamb as if he were on a spotlighted stage. It was a moment I would have missed if I'd stayed stuck comparing myself to everyone around me.

There will *always* be someone with more experience, flashier results, or a faster path to success. But comparison is an exhausting trap. It keeps you stuck in *everyone else's* narrative instead of focusing on your own. Instead of letting comparison paralyze you, reframe it. Let it push you to explore your own strengths, your own perspective, and your own path. The following sections provide a few steps to help you do just that.

Shift from Comparison to Inspiration

When you find yourself in awe of someone else's work or achievements, instead of thinking, *I'll never be that good*, ask yourself, "What can I learn from them?" Use their success as a spark for your own growth.

Example

If someone is an incredible public speaker, watch how they structure their presentations or engage the audience. Identify what resonates with you; then apply it to your own style.

Focus on Your Distinct Angle

Focus on what makes you unique—maybe it's a creative approach, the way you connect with people, or the way you communicate.

Exercise

Write down three things you bring to the table that are uniquely yours. Keep this list as a reminder when self-doubt creeps in.

Get Out of the Dugout

Sometimes, the best opportunities come when you step outside your comfort zone. Instead of staying in the space where you're comparing yourself to others, take action to create your own "winning shot."

Example

If you're intimidated by a team of seasoned colleagues, identify an area where you can bring value. Propose a project, offer to lead a task, or volunteer for something that aligns with your strengths.

Celebrate Progress, Not Perfection

Every time you focus on someone else's highlight reel, remind yourself that you're seeing their polished result, not the process or time it took to get there. Your path might look different, but that doesn't make it any less valid.

Exercise

At the end of each week, write down one win (big or small!) that you're proud of. Think about what you did to achieve it and how it aligns with your strengths.

Own Your Strengths; Don't Apologize for Them

In my opinion, *owning* your strengths is one of the toughest parts of truly embracing them. We often minimize our abilities, downplay our successes, or (worse yet) apologize for them. Whether it's due to imposter syndrome, self-doubt, or a fear of coming across as arrogant or cocky, we second-guess ourselves and make excuses for what we're good at.

But when you downplay your strengths, you are doing a disservice to yourself and the people who need you and your talents. The world doesn't need you to shrink. The world needs you to unapologetically show up as the best version of yourself.

Embrace Power Cues and Affirmations

One way to start owning your strengths is through physical cues and affirmations. For example, think about your body language. Even something as simple as sitting up straighter, if possible, can help. Try power cues before meetings or when you're about to present something important. Stand tall, take up space, and say to yourself, "I'm here for a reason. I bring something valuable to the table. I'm going to crush this."

Affirmations similarly can be very powerful. Examples of affirmations around your strengths include the following:

- I am a natural problem-solver, and I trust my ability to navigate complex situations.

- I am creative, and my ideas have the power to transform.

- I bring unique perspectives to any team I work with.

It might feel weird or awkward at first, but affirming your strengths aloud will help you internalize them. Try saying them in the mirror each morning, writing them down in a journal, or repeating them before big moments. The key is consistency. Over time, what you tell yourself becomes what you believe.

Begin to Overcome Your Fear of Success

My best friend, Gabby, recently started landing speaking gigs at conferences and on podcasts. She's been working in her field for a while now, quietly building a reputation as someone who's incredibly good at what she does. But when the invites started rolling in, her feelings of pride and excitement quickly gave way to fear and anxiety.

Before her first speaking session, we had a long conversation. "I don't know if I can do this," she admitted. "The other speaker has way more experience than I do. What if I get up there and mess up?"

I reminded her of what she already knew deep down: these opportunities didn't come out of nowhere. They're the direct result of years of hard work, expertise, and a proven track record. But no matter how much I reassured her, she couldn't shake the self-doubt.

What struck me most about that conversation was how deeply uncomfortable success felt for her. It wasn't that Gabby didn't want to succeed. She just wasn't sure if she was *ready* for what that success asked of her: the visibility, attention, and possibility for criticism. And she's not alone.

Why We Fear Success

Even when we've worked hard to embrace our strengths, our skills, and our backgrounds, many of us find ourselves hesitating when success finally comes knocking. Why? Because success often comes with a price: more responsibility, higher expectations, and a spotlight that can feel unnervingly bright.

We tend to think of fear as something that only holds us back from failure. But fear of success is just as real and just as paralyzing.

What if stepping into our power means losing the comfort of invisibility? What if it invites criticism or exposes us to vulnerability? These are tough questions, and they can lead us to self-sabotage, even when success is exactly what we've been striving for.

But success is about giving yourself the space to shine and contribute. And even if you stumble or fall short, it doesn't take away every future opportunity.

Reframe the Fear

When we fear success, we often conflate it with perfection. Basically, *If I succeed, I can't ever fail* or, *This is my one shot. Everything has to be perfect.* But that's not true. Success has nothing to do with being immune to mistakes or missteps. It means you've earned an opportunity to grow, learn, and make an impact.

When I feel overwhelmed or paralyzed by fear, I use a method called *fear-setting* to confront my doubts and reshape my thinking. If you're wrestling with self-doubt like Gabby was, here's how to try it:

1. *Define your fear.* Write down exactly what you're afraid of. Be specific. Is it the fear of public failure? Of being criticized? Of feeling (or looking) unprepared? Naming your fear makes it less abstract and more tangible.

2. *Think about the worst-case scenario.* Awful, I know. But ask yourself, "What's the absolute worst thing that could happen if I fail?" Be honest. Write it down. Then ask, "If that happened, what could I do to recover?" You'll often realize that even the worst-case scenario isn't as catastrophic as it seems. And even if it's particularly awful, there's a way to salvage it.

3. *List the potential upsides.* Think about what could go *right*. If you step into this opportunity, what might you gain?

How might this opportunity open doors, expand your network, or build your confidence?

4. *Identify a safety net.* What resources, people, or strategies could help you navigate any challenges that arise? Knowing you have support or a fallback plan can make stepping forward feel less daunting.

5. *Set a small, brave step.* You don't have to dive in headfirst. Identify one small, actionable step you can take to move forward. For Gabby, it was practicing her opening lines for her panel. For you, it might be sending that pitch or saying yes to a new project.

Before diving into the exercise, it helps to take a step back and reframe your perspective. Instead of getting stuck in worst-case-scenario thinking, let's break it down logically. Ask yourself:

What's the worst-case scenario if I fully embrace my strengths and succeed?	What are you most afraid might happen? *Be honest and specific.*
What's the best-case scenario?	Imagine the possibilities if everything went right. How might your life, career, and/or confidence grow?
What's the most likely outcome?	Most of the time, the most likely outcome lies somewhere in the middle: not as catastrophic as the worst-case scenario, but not necessarily as magical as the best-case either. Understanding this balance can be grounding.

Identifying and Embracing Your Strengths

When Gabby stepped onstage for her first panel, she still felt nervous. But she showed up anyway. She delivered her message, connected with the audience, and proved to herself that she was more than capable. Success didn't come once she erased her fear. It came from choosing courage over comfort.

For you, the journey might look different, but the principle is the same. Fear is not your enemy. It might just be a sign that you're stepping into something bigger than you've done before. And that's a good thing.

Takeaways

- Recognizing your strengths is about knowing what you're good at, embracing your strengths fully and without hesitation, and refusing to minimize them.
- Your strengths are what make you uniquely qualified for success. Use them strategically to create opportunities and drive growth.
- When you begin to step into your power and leverage your strengths, it can feel uncomfortable. Embrace the discomfort and analyze the situation to prepare accordingly.

Chapter 4

Building Your Circle: Mentors, Sponsors, and the Power of Community

No one thrives in isolation.

For a long time, I convinced myself I could figure everything out on my own. I mean, Google's free, right? But thriving in your career (or life) often depends on the people you surround yourself with. Mentors and community can be the secret ingredients that help you grow, stay grounded, and reach levels that you might not have thought possible.

Mentors can help you navigate challenges and make informed decisions, share hard-earned wisdom that you might not get from a blog post or podcast, and offer encouragement when things feel impossible.

And communities provide a sense of belonging, accountability, and opportunities. Finding like-minded people can make a world of difference, and being around driven people can open doors, motivate you to keep pushing forward, and help you think bigger.

My Crash Course in Confidence

When I landed one of my first full-time jobs, I stepped into a sink-or-swim environment. On top of that, I didn't really know what mentorship was or why it even mattered.

My manager at the time saw something in me that I couldn't yet see in myself. While my last manager basically handed me a list of KPIs (key performance indicators) and sent me on my way, this one chose to coach me through the big stuff:

- How to advocate for myself.
- How to think critically about business strategy and how my work impacted the larger company goals.
- How to bounce back when a campaign or project flopped.

He didn't sugarcoat feedback or let me off the hook, but he also never let me fail alone. That balance of tough love and unwavering support shaped my career *and* built my confidence.

Today, I mentor college students and young professionals, and I get to see it from the other side. Watching someone's eyes light up as they connect the dots or gain clarity on their next move is its own kind of magic.

That's the power of mentorship: it's transformative on both sides.

Distinguish Between Mentors and Sponsors (What's the Difference Anyway?)

Before we dive into how to find a mentor, it's important to remember that mentorship and sponsorship aren't the same thing. Both are invaluable, but they serve different roles in your growth. (Refer to Table 4.1.)

Put another way:

- A mentor helps you prepare for the race.
- A sponsor gets you on the track.

Ideally, you'll have both mentors and sponsors (and some people can fill both roles), but mentors are usually the starting point.

Table 4.1 Mentor Versus Sponsor

Mentor	Sponsor
Provides guidance and advice	Advocates for you in professional settings
Helps you grow your skills and confidence	(Potentially) Puts their reputation on the line to open doors for you
Helps you figure out what you want	Helps you get it
(Typically) Focuses on your personal and professional development	(Typically) Focuses on your career advancement
Guides, advises, and offers perspective	Advocates for you; says your name in rooms you're not in; pushes for you to get that promotion or big opportunity

Find the Right Mentor

A lot of people think finding a mentor means approaching the most successful person you know and asking for a formal mentor/mentee relationship.

Don't do that.

The best mentors are people whose experiences align with your goals *and* who genuinely care about helping you succeed. Here's how to find the right mentor without making it awkward.

Be Clear About What You Need

Before you start looking, figure out what you actually need help with. Are you navigating a career or industry pivot? Do you need help advocating for yourself? Are you struggling with confidence? Or maybe you want guidance on entrepreneurship and building your own thing. Whatever the reason, mentorship works best when it's intentional.

As you consider what you need, be sure to include the following:

- What skills, knowledge, or guidance you're looking for.
- What kind of experience or perspective you'd value in a mentor.
- What you hope to gain from the relationship.

Build the Relationship Organically

Walking up to someone and saying, "Will you be my mentor?" feels weird. Because it is. Instead, start with a conversation:

- Ask for their insights on a challenge you're facing.
- Engage with their content (if they post online).
- Send a thoughtful message about how their work has inspired you.

Recently, I hopped on a call with Morgan J. Ingram, founder of AMP Social, who helps B2B (business-to-business) leaders turn their expertise into predictable revenue and pipeline through LinkedIn. He articulated it best:

> We're just afraid to ask for help because we think people look down on us, but you'd be surprised how happy people are to share their knowledge with you. So this is how you ask for help: never say you want to pick someone's brain—that just sounds disgusting and painful. Instead, approach it like this: "I'm looking to learn [specific skill] and accelerate my learning. What would it take to get a month of your time to walk me through this?"

Notice I said, "What would it take?" You need to approach people knowing that their time is valuable. If you just say, "Can I pick your brain?" then I know you're going to waste my time asking things you could've Googled. And chances are, you're also not going to do what I told you to do, which will piss me off even more.

But if you say, "I've been working on this, I have some understanding, but I know you're great at it and I want to accelerate my learning—what would it take to work with you?" That's all you need to do.

His advice is simple but powerful. Be intentional, respect people's time, and show that you're serious about learning.

Find Your Community

After finding the right mentor, the next step is to find the community that is right for you. This step did not come easily for me. When I first set out to find a professional community, it felt like some awful form of speed-dating. I joined groups for marketers, women in business, and people of color in tech. Some were too formal, others drained my energy, and some required way more engagement than I could handle.

At one point, I was a member of 16 (!) Slack communities. As an introvert who sometimes struggles to text her own friends back, that was way too much.

Today, I'm part of a select number of communities and groups that inspire me, challenge me, and help me improve my craft. The key was figuring out what I needed *before* seeking out communities to join. Because just like mentorship, finding the right community is about alignment with your goals, personality, and values.

Table 4.2   Community Fit Checklist

Criteria	Community A	Community B	Community C
Aligns with my values	Yes	No	Yes
Offers resources	Yes	Yes	No
Involves active engagement	Yes	Yes	Yes
Prioritizes inclusivity	No	Yes	Yes

As you begin your journey to finding your own community, ask yourself the following questions:

- What do I hope to gain from this community?
- Do I prefer in-person gatherings or online spaces?
- How much time and energy can I realistically commit (per day, week, month, etc.)?

You can use this table to track and evaluate potential communities; refer to Table 4.2.

Whether it's a mentor who helps you navigate uncharted waters or a community that helps you become better in your chosen field, both can serve as catalysts for growth. They not only guide you but also push you to achieve more than you thought possible.

Build Your Own Community When You Can't Find One

There's a lot of advice out there about finding a professional community. *Join a Slack group. Sign up for a Discord channel. Go to networking events.* And sure, sometimes that works! But what if the spaces you're trying to force yourself into don't actually … fit? What if none of them feel right?

My good friend Tobi Oluwole, co-founder of Magnate and the Founder's Blueprint, framed it in a way that completely shifted my perspective. Instead of constantly searching for a new community to join, he suggested something else: *build one.*

> I think community is very effective in groups of like six to ten people, which you don't necessarily need to be part of a movement for. [When I started our LinkedIn creators' group], I just sent a text to you and a few other people like, "Yo, let's hang out once a month." And I think more people just need to take the initiative. Your most powerful asset as a human being is your ability to create whatever you desire.[1]

Tobi has built multiple impactful communities, but he keeps it simple: *find people you enjoy spending time with and build around that.* And there's so much freedom in this. You don't have to mold yourself to fit into a group that wasn't designed with you in mind. You don't have to "network" the way people expect you to. If the right space for you doesn't exist, you can create it.

And that doesn't mean launching some big, monetized membership or starting a movement. It can be as simple as curating a group of people who inspire and challenge you.

"I think we always try to convince people that they can fit in somewhere," he told me. "A lot of people *don't* fit in anywhere. My company, all of my hires, are all misfits. My financial controller is a 22-year-old farm girl that built a whole company. You can build what you really, really want. And it doesn't have to be big. You don't have to start a movement. You don't have to monetize it. You can just hang out with people that you like. That's what life is really about."

53

It's easy to forget that when we're caught up in a corporate bubble, a LinkedIn bubble, or any entrepreneurship bubble. We tell ourselves that community is about strategy or visibility, but at the core, it's about connection. For most of us, it's about

- surrounding ourselves with people we like, trust, and respect;
- having fun and learning together;
- and yeah, getting paid while we do it.

But when you focus too much on the last one, you can forget how important the first two are. The best communities don't require you to contort yourself to fit in. They're built around genuine connection, aligned values, and people who just get you.

And if you don't have that yet, you can create it.

Takeaways

- The right mentor helps you think bigger, advocate for yourself, and navigate challenges and new opportunities with confidence. Find someone whose experience aligns with your goals and who *genuinely* wants to see you win.
- Join communities that energize, not drain, you. The best communities push you to grow and feel like a natural fit. Instead of forcing yourself into every group, be intentional. Are you choosing spaces that align with your values and ambitions?
- Give before you take. Whether in mentorship or community, actively showing up, sharing your insights and experiences, and adding value makes all the difference. The more you contribute, the more you'll get in return.

Chapter 5

Deciding If a Portfolio Career Is Right for You

In the early years of building my career, I tried to follow the conventional advice that everyone seemed to be shouting from the rooftops: "Find one thing to specialize in and become the best at it."

And sure, for some people, this advice works beautifully. But for me, it felt like I was trying to shove a square peg into a round hole. It was awkward, deeply unfulfilling, and draining.

At the time, I thought my struggle was a personal failure; yet I wasn't unfocused or indecisive. I just hadn't yet realized that I was *multi-passionate*. A multi-passionate person (or a multi-potentialite) is someone with a wide range of skills and interests that don't fit neatly into a career path. The first time I heard this term, everything clicked. I had varied skills and interests that didn't fit into a singular job title. And honestly, why should they?

Contrary to what I believed, I wasn't failing. I was simply operating outside a single-track career model. That's where the concept of a portfolio career comes in.

What the Heck Is a Portfolio Career?

A *portfolio career* is a career model built around *multiple* income streams, skills, and roles. With a portfolio career, you do not tie your identity (and paycheck) to just one job. Think of it like diversifying your career the way you would a financial portfolio. Each "career asset" contributes to a bigger, more resilient whole.

Or picture it this way: Imagine you're an art gallery owner, but this time, you're curating a gallery of your own work. Each piece represents a skill, passion, or revenue stream that contributes to the whole.

Some people have a full-time job and add on a few creative projects or side gigs. Others build a patchwork of part-time roles, freelance work, and passion projects, none of which are "the one." The beauty of a portfolio career is that it's entirely yours to define. Here are some examples:

- A recruiter who also freelances as a career coach, speaks at HR conferences, and runs a job search newsletter.

- A consultant who splits time between brand strategy, writing, and public speaking.

- A graphic designer who also owns an e-commerce brand and does corporate trainings on design and branding.

When I finally embraced this career model, everything started to make a lot more sense for me. I didn't have to choose one path. I could do the things I cared about and make it work *my way*.

Why Portfolio Careers Are on the Rise

We're in an era where people are redefining work on their own terms. The question is, why? Multiple reasons address this question:

- Traditional job security is no longer guaranteed. Layoffs, industry shifts, and a tumultuous economy have made income diversification a smart strategy. For a lot of people, it's no longer a nice-to-have. It's a necessity.

- People want more autonomy and flexibility, meaning more control over their schedules, workloads, and the type of work they do. A portfolio career offers freedom and independence in a way that many traditional jobs do not.

- Professional success isn't solely defined by climbing a corporate ladder anymore. It's also about building careers that reflect our skills, values, and interests.

We can seek meaning and fulfillment in our careers, but that doesn't mean we're willing to compromise financial stability. The idea of "stability" is changing. Why depend on one employer for 100% of your income or one job for professional satisfaction when a portfolio career allows you to spread your risk and creativity across multiple revenue streams?

Identify What You Need to Know Before Diving In

Before you commit to this path, there are a few things you should know. The earlier you wrap your head around these truths, the less pressure you'll feel to have it all figured out from day one. It won't guarantee a smooth ride, but it *will* make the bumps less surprising.

- You don't have to monetize everything. Just because you're good at something doesn't mean it has to become a business. Be intentional.

- Test the waters before making any big moves. I didn't quit my job one day and start a business the next. I experimented with different revenue streams before transitioning fully. It's okay to start with one freelance project, course, or gig to see if it's a good fit.

- Some things will not work out. That is okay, and that is to be expected. I tried photography, e-commerce, consulting, and writing before I figured out what was sustainable for me.

- Your career will evolve. What works for you now might shift over time. Be open to changing directions as you grow.

Ask Yourself Whether You Are Built for a Portfolio Career

A portfolio career isn't for everyone, and that's okay. Some people thrive in the structure of a single, full-time role. (Refer to Table 5.1.)

But if the idea of blending multiple skills, roles, and income streams excites you, the best way to start is to identify the skills you'd like to monetize, understand your ideal workday, and find your "why."

Conduct a Skill Audit

A portfolio career works best when you leverage the right combination of skills. But how do you figure out which ones to focus on?

Table 5.1 Portfolio Career Pros and Cons

Pros	Cons
Creative freedom and variety in your work	Requires excellent time and project management skills
Resilience through diversified income	Can feel overwhelming to juggle roles; can be prone to burnout
Opportunities to monetize multiple skills	Income unpredictable at times
Autonomy over your schedule and projects	Lacks the stability (or structure) of a single employer

Table 5.2 Finding the Right Combination of Skills

Skills I Enjoy Using	Areas I'm Highly Skilled In	Skills I Can Get Paid For

Create a three-column table as shown in Table 5.2.

Look for skills that appear in all three columns. These are likely your sweet spot skills that will offer both fulfillment and income potential.

Figure Out Your Ideal Workday

Your day-to-day work structure matters just as much as your skills. And a portfolio career requires self-management, so understanding your ideal work rhythm is key—not just for productivity but also for sustainability.

Write down your ideal workday in detail. Think about:

- What time do you wake up and start working?
- What types of tasks energize you?
- Do you prefer working solo or collaborating?
- How much flexibility do you want in your schedule?

Then compare your answers to your current reality. If your dream day looks nothing like your actual day, and building that ideal setup feels unrealistic or stressful, it might be worth reconsidering this path. A portfolio career is about doing work you enjoy or love, but it's also about designing a lifestyle that works *for* you, not just looks good on paper.

Would this kind of structure actually support the way you want to live and work, or would it stretch you too thin?

Decide If a Portfolio Career Fits Alongside Your Full-time Job

Before diving into a portfolio career, you need to ask yourself: *Can this fit alongside my 9-to-5 right now?*

Not just in terms of time, but in terms of energy, priorities, and capacity. Some roles leave room for creative projects or side income. Others demand so much from you that even the thought of doing anything else feels exhausting. Neither is wrong. You just need to be honest about what season you're in. This is the time to have a really honest conversation with yourself about your job's flexibility, your manager's expectations, and how much mental bandwidth you actually have outside of work. Are you chasing something that energizes you, or are you piling on an already full plate?

When I started exploring portfolio work and intentionally building this type of career for myself, it wasn't exactly a smooth leap into a new career. There were times when I needed to scale back other projects to focus on my full-time job. At times, especially at the beginning, managers questioned my ability to prioritize. Their concerns weren't entirely unfounded either. Balancing multiple income streams and ventures can be daunting.

My 9-to-5 was my safety net. It provided healthcare and benefits I couldn't live without, the (relatively) stable paycheck that covered my essentials, and the structure that allowed me to explore other opportunities without the overwhelming pressure of immediate financial success.

And let me be clear, I still prioritized my full-time role. I *wanted* to excel in my role because I knew that it gave me the foundation to sharpen my skills and build everything else on top of it. Learning how to balance my 9-to-5 while layering in additional income streams was a game-changer.

So, if you're considering this career path while holding onto your full-time job, you should understand that the two *can* coexist and thrive together. But it requires ruthless organization, time management, and honesty—with yourself and, if necessary, with your employer.

Recognize That You Don't Have to Quit Right Away (or Ever)

As we discussed earlier in this chapter, pursuing a portfolio career doesn't have to mean quitting your job cold turkey. In fact, for many people, a full-time role is one part of their portfolio, and a very necessary one. It can be the foundation that makes the rest possible.

Plenty of folks start layering on freelance work, creative projects, or side hustles while keeping their day job. It's a smart way to mitigate risk, get clear on what actually works, *and* experiment without the pressure to make everything click immediately. But before you start juggling multiple things, remember that there is no one-size-fits-all formula here. The goal doesn't have to be to escape your 9-to-5 at all costs. It can be to create a career that feels aligned, sustainable, and uniquely yours.

That said, *wanting* that kind of career and *being ready* to build it are two different things. You've got to check in with yourself first— your time, your energy, and your capacity.

Assess Your Bandwidth

Let's be real. Adding extra work on top of a full-time job isn't easy. The first step is to evaluate your capacity, both in terms of time and mental energy.

Ask yourself three questions and take note of your answers:

1. *Am I consistently drained at the end of the day, or do I have energy for something new?* Taking on more will demand a reserve of energy you might not even realize you're depleting.

2. *Do I have pockets of time to focus on a side project (evenings, weekend, even lunch breaks)?* Maybe it's a quiet evening when you'd otherwise be doomscrolling or a weekend morning you can dedicate to productivity. Even small windows of time add up.

3. *Can I carve out a few hours of week without overwhelming myself?* A portfolio career requires focus, discipline, and creativity. If your full-time role is leaving you mentally fried, you'll need to figure out if you have enough left in you to dedicate to other ventures. This doesn't mean you have to dive headfirst into a second job. It might just mean carving out an hour here or there to experiment without overloading yourself.

> **Tip:** Start small. You don't have to jump in at full speed. Devote a couple of hours a week (if possible) to test the waters. That way, you can gauge how it feels and how well you can manage, without committing too much too soon.

Review Your Employment Agreements

A few years back, a former colleague excitedly announced her new side hustle online. She was met with congratulations, new leads … and a meeting with HR added to her calendar. Within the week, she'd been let go. The reason: she was not actually allowed to have a side hustle.

The excitement of starting a side hustle can fizzle quickly if you run into employment restrictions. Some companies limit outside work, and the last thing you want is to get hit with legal trouble or dismissal.

Some things to consider:

- *Noncompete clauses:* Will your side work conflict with your job?
- *Moonlighting policies:* Are you allowed to take on outside work (in general)? Do you need to disclose it?
- *Confidentiality agreements:* Be extra cautious about projects that could overlap with your job's proprietary information or client relationships. Even unintentional breaches of confidentiality can land you in hot water.

The key here: transparency. Ask HR or review your contract before launching into anything new.

Start with the Low-hanging Fruit

One of the hardest parts of building a portfolio career is knowing where to begin. The good news is that you don't have to reinvent the wheel. Instead of chasing high-risk ideas that require a ton of upfront work or funding, start with what's already within reach. Revisit the skill audit you did earlier and look for overlap in these areas:

- *Skills you're confident in:* What do you know you're good at, either from experience or training?
- *Things people already ask you for help with:* What do coworkers, friends, or clients naturally turn to you for?
- *Services or products you could offer with minimal setup:* What could you realistically launch in a few hours a week without needing to invest a ton of time or money?

My good friend Aleah Roseen has a great job in auto insurance. And during the pandemic, she picked up a new hobby: baking bread. Three years later, she started selling it as a side hustle. As she tells it:

> The one-year mark isn't even when I started my actual business—it was just when I first *considered* selling to other people. It was all word of mouth—[my fiancée's] coworkers or people I played recreational sports with, people I was close with. I would make it as gifts, and then people started saying, "Oh my gosh, you should sell this, it's really good."
>
> At first, I wondered, "Would people even buy it?" But my friends were really supportive and started paying me for it. That's when I thought, "Okay, maybe I can take this a bit broader."[1]

A year after that, she named her business *Rustic Crust*, built a website, and kept at it. While it's not her full-time job, she's taking it day by day, year by year, with no pressure to go all in right away.

That's the key. Start small. Often, the simplest ideas make the best entry point. You don't have to overcomplicate it by chasing something shiny or high stakes right out the gate. Focus on traction first. Then you can build, test, and evolve from there.

Preparing Your Finances

Let's talk money.

It can be one of the biggest sticking points when people consider a portfolio career. *How much will I actually make? Can I sustain myself long-term? What happens if one of my income streams dries up?* These are all valid concerns, and they're worth addressing before you make any big moves.

My Leap into the Unknown

When I decided to leave corporate and launch my own business, my biggest fear was finances—namely, financial instability. Having a steady paycheck felt like a security blanket, and the idea of giving that up was terrifying and thrilling. Thrilling because I'd finally have the freedom to build something on my terms; terrifying because ... bills.

To start, I leaned heavily on my business coach, my therapist, and my partner to help me untangle the anxiety that came with this. I worked on reframing my fears, challenging my mindset around scarcity and not being able to provide for myself, and reminding myself why I wanted to do this in the first place. The work I did to shift my mindset helped, but it wasn't enough on its own. I had to roll up my sleeves and get tactical.

I developed a financial plan that accounted for worst-case scenarios, adjusted my budget to reduce financial risk, and set clear income goals before going all-in. That preparation didn't erase all my fear, but it gave me the confidence to take the leap, knowing I wasn't just winging it.

If financial uncertainty is keeping you from exploring a portfolio career, you're not alone. The good news: There are practical steps you can take to minimize risk and build confidence in your financial stability.

Define Financial Stability for Yourself

Financial stability looks different for everyone. For some, it means having a steady, predictable income that covers their bills. For others, it's about diversification and knowing that if one revenue stream dips, they have another to fall back on.

To get clarity, start by defining what financial stability means *for you*. This will require you to get honest about your current expenses, your desired lifestyle, and the kind of buffer you need to feel secure.

Table 5.3   Calculating Financial Stability

Category	Expense	Monthly Cost	Notes
Essentials	*Rent/Mortgage*		
	Groceries		
	Utilities		
	Daycare		
Personal Well-being	*Therapy*		
	Subscriptions		
Savings and Buffer	*Savings*		
	"Fun" Expenses		

Instead of aiming for an arbitrary income goal, reverse-engineer your numbers based on what you actually need.

To calculate this, you can use Table 5.3.

Add up your essential expenses: rent or mortgage, utilities, groceries, insurance, debt payments, etc. Then factor in your "nice-to-have" expenses, like dining out, subscriptions, or travel.

Then take a step back and evaluate what's truly necessary and what you could scale back if needed. *(Remember, this won't last forever!)* Then, finally, include a buffer for savings and emergencies because even the best-laid plans need room to breathe.

Once you have that full picture, you'll have a clearer sense of your "enough" number and whether your current income streams can support it or if you need to adjust.

Identify Your Risk Tolerance

Portfolio careers can feel riskier than a 9-to-5, for sure, but diversification can actually provide built-in stability. You're able to spread your income across multiple sources rather than relying on one paycheck, which can help soften any financial blows. *But* you still need to consider your risk tolerance.

Ask yourself:

- Am I comfortable with fluctuating income?
- Do I have savings to cushion slower months?
- Would I prefer to build my portfolio career alongside a part-time or full-time job at first?

Your answers can shift over time, just like your career. But know where you stand now, so you can make informed financial decisions as you build.

Take It One Bill at a Time

Thinking big picture can be overwhelming, especially when it comes to money. If the idea of replacing your *entire* salary or hitting a huge monthly income goal feels daunting, you're not alone! So, try zooming in instead. Break down your financial goals by individual expenses.

One trick that's always helped me is assigning specific expenses to specific income streams. So instead of thinking, *I need to make an extra $3,000 this month*, try this:

- *I want this client's retainer to cover my rent.*
- *I want this freelance project to cover my groceries.*
- *I want this speaking gig to go into savings.*

The nice thing about this approach is that it helps make financial planning feel more tangible and *way* less intimidating. We're not looking to magically solve everything all at once—we're building confidence and momentum, one step at a time.

Here's how to reframe your income goals in a way that feels grounded and actionable:

- **Assign each income stream to a specific expense.**

  Whether it's a side gig, freelance project, course launch, etc., give that income a clear purpose. It turns abstract money goals into real-life wins.

- **Add a buffer for savings and unexpected costs.**

  Don't just plan for the ideal or best-case scenario. Life happens. Build some flexibility into your plan so one hiccup doesn't have the power to derail everything.

- **Track and adjust monthly.**

  What worked? What didn't? Are there new expenses or revenue streams to account for? Your plan should evolve as you, and your career, do.

And here's the best part: when you hit the smaller milestones, you start to trust yourself more. You realize you *can* do it. You *can* make this work, step by step. Before you know it, you'll be setting (and smashing) bigger goals but without being overwhelmed.

There's no single blueprint for building a portfolio career. Just a series of choices, experience, and lessons that guide you along the way. Some seasons will feel slow. Others will stretch you in ways you didn't expect. But every step you take will bring you closer to something more aligned, more flexible, and more *you*.

Whether you're easing in with a side hustle or taking a full leap into self-employment, remember that you don't have to chase perfection. The goal should be sustainability. It's about giving yourself permission to build a career on your own terms, one bill, one project, one season at a time.

You don't need to have it all figured out to begin. But if you've made it this far, you're already more ready than you think.

Takeaways

- A portfolio career is more than a backup plan. It's a proactive way to build stability, flexibility, and creative fulfillment. Whether you're driven by financial goals, a desire for more freedom, or even the need to explore different parts of yourself, this model will allow you to design a career on your terms.
- You don't have to walk away from a full-time job in order to embrace a portfolio career. Many people start by layering in freelance work or side gigs before making any major moves, and others never leave their 9-to-5 at all. You get to set the pace and your goals.
- Preparation gives you options. Knowing your "enough" number, assessing your bandwidth, and planning for real expenses helps you take more confident risks and recover from setbacks without spiraling.

Chapter 6

Building a Purposeful Portfolio Career

If you finished the last chapter and thought, *Yes! This portfolio career thing might be for me,* first of all, welcome. I'm thrilled you're here. Second, let's talk about what comes next.

Once you've made the decision to step off the traditional path and start building a career that's more … you-shaped, there's a bit of a learning curve. By "a bit," I mean some days will feel like you're soaring, life has never been better, and you're *definitely* on the right track. Other days, it'll feel like you've somehow forgotten to use a calendar, don't know what you're doing, and should give up.

Don't worry! All of this is to be expected. You don't have to subscribe to a one-size-fits-all strategy, but there is a process. And in this chapter, we'll walk through it.

Normalize the Chaos (You're Not Alone!)

Let's start with the question that stumps multi-passionates and multi-hyphenates everywhere:

"So … what do you do for a living?"

Cue the awkward laugh, the five-job-title monologues, and the glazed-over eyes of the person who asked.

If your work spans multiple roles, industries, or income streams, you've probably had this moment. I, for one, have experienced this more times than I care to admit. That moment when your career stops fitting into a LinkedIn headline or a one-liner at a networking event. When your own elevator pitch feels like a TED Talk. And that moment can feel … a little disorienting.

But the truth is, just because your path is unconventional doesn't mean it's unclear. It's *yours*. And the more you own that, the easier it becomes to talk about, and build on, what you do.

As portfolio careerists, we're not building around a single title. We're building a body of work.

Define Success and Purpose (So You Don't Burn Out Chasing Someone Else's)

For those of us with nontraditional careers, success isn't handed to us in a neat little package. And when you don't have a boss setting your goals, a clear promotion track, or performance reviews telling you where to focus, it's up to *you* to define success. If you don't, the algorithm, or your peers' highlight reels, will gladly do it for you.

So, let's not wing it. Let's define it.

Start with the Why

You might've touched on this in Chapter 5 when you did your skill audit and identified what lights you up. Now, let's take it further. Ask yourself:

- What kind of impact do I want to have?
- What do I want my work to make possible—for me and for others?
- When do I feel the *most proud* of what I've built?

For Linda Le, her mindset shift came down to one core value: freedom. "I wanted to be able to live life on my terms, and I knew in order to do that, I had to be willing to step outside my comfort zone," she explained. "My mindset was constantly, *You have nothing to lose but everything to gain.*"[1]

For me, my "why" came down to three things:

- Financial freedom, so I could build wealth on my own terms.
- Creative freedom, so I could work on projects that excite me.
- Joy, so I could wake up and feel fulfilled by the bigger picture.

If a project didn't support at least one of those, it was a no. (Okay, fine, sometimes it was a "maybe later.")

Exercise: Write Out Your "Why"

Take a few minutes to reflect. Then write a short "why" statement that you can keep visible when making career decisions.

Here are some examples to get you started:

- My why is being able to provide for my family without worrying about bills.
- My why is to pursue both an athletic and an intellectual career path without sacrificing either.

Set Your Own Metrics

No one's handing you the keys to a corner office or a gold watch for 30 years of loyalty (unless you buy it for yourself). You need to define your own milestones. Try setting two or three metrics that actually matter to you. Something like:

- I want 60% of my income to come from creative projects.
- I want to work no more than 30 hours a week.
- I want to be able to say "yes" to clients who respect my boundaries and whose work lights me up, and be able to say "no" to the rest.

These goals can (and will!) evolve. Check in with yourself at least quarterly. Your "why" today might shift tomorrow—and that's a feature, not a bug.

Structure Your Career (So It Doesn't Swallow You Whole)

Ah, freedom. Glorious, chaotic freedom.

Portfolio careers promise you a lot of it, and flexibility too. But let's be real. Without structure, flexibility can feel like a never-ending, self-directed group project with no due dates. I'm not saying you need to set up rigid systems and never shift. But you *do* need to find your rhythm. So, let's build it.

Use the Three-Bucket Framework

Inspired by Adam Nash's product prioritization model, I created a framework that helps me stop jumping from task to task with zero strategy.

Here's how it works. Divide your work into three buckets:

1. *Revenue Drivers:* Client work, speaking engagements, anything that pays the bills.

2. *Growth Projects:* Things that might not pay (yet) but help you build long-term impact or value, like launching a new offering or creating content.

3. *Joy Projects:* The work that fills your cup; basically, anything that excites you, rejuvenates you, or brings you back to *why* you started building this career in the first place. For me, that includes mentorship, writing, and creative side projects.

Check in on your buckets once a month. Ask yourself:

- Where is most of my time and energy going?
- What's missing?
- Which buckets are overflowing?
- Which projects still feel aligned, and which feel like dead weight?

If everything's falling into Revenue and nothing else, you risk burnout. If everything's a Joy project, but your bank account is gasping for air, that's your cue to shift focus a bit. The goal isn't perfect balance all day every day but awareness. The buckets will help you make intentional trade-offs and make sure you're building something sustainable, not just busy.

Build a Weekly Flow That Works for You

Forget the rigid 9-to-5. You're building something for *you*. But like I mentioned earlier, flexibility can turn into chaos fast if you don't give it some structure.

To be clear, you don't need to schedule every minute of your day (unless you're like me and you love a time-blocked, color-coded calendar; then you do you). But a consistent, weekly rhythm can help you stay focused without burning out.

Here's how to start:

- *List everything that's on your plate.* I'm talking client work, your full-time job (if applicable), admin tasks, creative projects, therapy. Even dog walks.

- *Batch similar tasks together.* If you find that you're constantly bouncing between strategy, creative work, and emails, your brain is probably begging for a break. Try grouping tasks: admin in the mornings, deep work in the afternoons, creative blocks after your walk. Whatever works for your energy. Now, task-batching isn't a one-size-fits-all solution. So, if it doesn't work for you, tweak it. The goal here is to find a rhythm that actually supports your focus and flow.

- *Take a step back and look at the flow.* Is it giving you structure and breathing room? Or does it still feel chaotic?

If it helps, think of your week like a playlist. You want a mix of tracks to help you focus, tracks to help you rest and recover, and a few hits that just make you feel good. If every day is focused on hustle and productivity, you're just asking for burnout.

Protect Your Energy (Because Boundaries Aren't Optional)

Early in my career, I treated boundaries like something reserved only for rich people with assistants. You know, the kind of people who say things like, "Circle back with me next quarter," while sipping a smoothie.

I was not one of those people. I was trying to build credibility. I wanted to prove I was real. So, I said yes to everything. Accepted every request for a coffee chat. Responded to emails on Sunday mornings while brushing my teeth. Accepted rush projects with 12-hour turnarounds and somehow convinced myself that I just thrived under pressure.

Spoiler alert: I didn't.

That kind of availability comes at a cost. And eventually, my relationships, mental health, and creativity took a hit. And worse, I had trained the people around me to expect my time, energy, and creativity on demand. My career was running me, not the other way around.

I was beyond frustrated.

But the real problem wasn't the people who had such demanding expectations. It was me. I had never clearly defined my own limits. No one was going to create boundaries for me. If I wanted work-life harmony, I was going to have to create it myself. What I've learned the hard way is that boundaries are about creating a system, life, and career that are all sustainable *for you*. They aren't necessarily about making yourself unavailable and inaccessible all the time. They're how you protect the work you actually want to do. They're how you make space for creativity, not just productivity. And they're how you train the people around you—clients, collaborators, even loved ones—to treat your time and energy with respect.

So, I did something that felt almost radical at the time: I created my *Personal Energy Protection Plan*, which is my system for defining and maintaining boundaries that give me structure and prevent burnout. So, let's give it a try.

Build Your Personal Energy Protection Plan

You don't need a fancy framework for this. You can start by asking yourself a few questions:

1. *What work energizes me, and what drains me?* Are there certain types of projects or tasks that fire you up? Do certain types of clients leave you feeling burnt out?

What Energizes and Drains Me?

Energizing	Draining

---

2. *When am I most productive, and when do I need breaks?* Identify your peak focus hours and define when you need nonnegotiable breaks. For me, my peak focus hours are 5 a.m.–10 a.m. and 4 p.m.–8 p.m. That doesn't mean I don't work during the day, but I know when I'll be the most focused and creative.

Productivity

Peak Focus Hours	Nonnegotiable Breaks

---

3. *What are my personal nonnegotiables?* Maybe it's no meetings before 9 a.m. Maybe you want to protect your weekends and spend as much time as possible with your family. Maybe it's 90-minute walks with your dog while listening to your favorite podcast (*or maybe that's just me?*). All of it counts.

4. *How do I want to handle client or team requests that exceed my capacity?* Try to write some of your scripts now so that you're not stuck scrambling later. Here are some ideas:

- Thanks for thinking of me! I'd love to help, but my calendar is full this week. Can we revisit next month?

- I'm offline after 6 p.m., but I'll make sure to get back to you first thing tomorrow.

- This sounds like a great opportunity, but it's outside my current focus. Let's keep the door open for future collaborations.

- Let's revisit this after the weekend. I'm happy to pick this up on Monday or Tuesday!

Personal Nonnegotiables

Daily Habits	Work Boundaries

Once you've got your answers, live by them. You don't have to announce your boundaries online, but they should be the scaffolding that holds your work together. And here's the part no one tells you: the right people will appreciate that you have boundaries. It shows that you value your time and, by extension, theirs. The ones who don't respect them were never your people to begin with.

Protect your peace. You didn't leave the traditional path just to rebuild chaos for yourself in a different form.

Find Joy in the Process (Even When It's a Mess)

Let's be real. This career path you're building isn't always going to be glamorous. You're not going to wake up every day with birds chirping outside your window and *The Greatest Showman* soundtrack playing in the background.

I've never subscribed to the idea that "If you love what you do, you'll never work a day in your life." Some days, the work is fulfilling. Other days, it's just … work. Emails, invoices, admin tasks, late-night projects, you name it. But joy doesn't have to be big, bold, or post-worthy to be real and worth celebrating.

Joy can look like this:

- Working with that one client who actually *gets* you, trusts you, and makes every project fun.

- The feeling of finishing a deliverable you're genuinely proud of.

- Creating something that makes you think, *Huh. I'm actually pretty damn good at this*.

- Taking a midday walk because your schedule allows it.

- Saying no to a project that doesn't align, and feeling the relief hit immediately.

I used to think joy had to be some grand passion or full-time calling. But over time, I've realized joy is often quieter. It's tucked into the pockets of your day: the work you lose track of time doing, the small wins, the way you feel when you get to be fully yourself in your work.

So, when the chaos hits (because it will), come back to that. What brings you joy, even in small doses? What part of your work makes you feel like *you*? Write it down. Keep it somewhere visible. Revisit it when the grind starts grinding a little too hard.

Joy might not always be loud, but it's what will keep you going when things get weird or busy.

Embrace the Ebbs and Flows (and Use Them Well)

Portfolio careers typically have a rhythm. And part of that rhythm is quiet.

You'll have seasons of high energy and opportunity. Launches that take off, clients rolling in, a calendar so full it makes you nostalgic for boredom. And then you'll have the ebbs. The slower stretches. Fewer emails, fewer meetings, more space than expected. For me, this typically happens over the summer. Events slow down (so less in-person speaking engagements) and most brands aren't leaping to onboard a new agency right before Independence Day.

But slow doesn't mean stagnant. It doesn't mean your momentum has disappeared. And it certainly doesn't mean that people have forgotten about you. It just means that you're between waves. And if you use it well, that in-between is where the next level gets built.

Early on, I used to be freaked out by the quiet seasons. I'd double- and triple-check my inbox like something must be broken. Refresh my LinkedIn DMs. Mentally scroll through recent posts wondering if I accidentally said something bad.

Now, I look at the slow seasons as the strategic breathing room that they are. These are the moments when you get to work *on* your business or career more, not just *in* it. These moments make the next wave possible.

Use the Lulls Like a Pro

Here's what to do when the pace slows down:

- *Audit and refine your offers.* A few questions you can ask yourself:
  - What's still working?
  - What's not quite hitting the mark?
  - What could be simplified or upgraded?
  - Is it time to update my pricing?

- *Reconnect with your "why."* When the calendar clears a bit, it's a great time to reflect on what you actually want to build next, not just what you've been reacting too.

- *Follow up with your network.* Past clients, collaborators, the people who always say, "Let's do something together!" and never schedule the call. Now's the time.

- *Up-level your skill set.* Is there a course you've been itching to take? A low-lift idea sitting in your Notes app that would make you stronger in your craft? Use this time to learn and experiment without the pressure of an immediate return.

- *Actually rest.* I mean it. Go offline. Read. Travel. Embrace hobbies that you usually don't have time for. And don't mistake rest for laziness—rest is what makes future momentum sustainable. We don't have to *earn* the right to rest.

Ray, a certified personal trainer and owner of Body by RayRay, said it best:

> Over the years, I have learned to embrace the ebbs and flows that comes with operating a small business and use the slower times as an opportunity to try new things. Offer new services, expand my community through various events and be willing to grow within my personal and business journey. It will still be really hard, even if you are insanely passionate about it. It is absolutely worth it though, and you will be so proud of yourself every time you hit any mark. At least, you should be![2]

It's easy to panic in the quiet, especially if you've been in a season of *go, go, go*. But oftentimes, the best growth I've had, both personally and professionally, has followed a slowdown. It's when

I've sat down, reimagined my services, clarified my strategy, or simply come back to work with fresh energy and perspectives.

So, if things feel still but you're in a good place financially, don't sprint to fill the space if you don't need to. Sit with it. Use it. Because when the next wave comes (and it always does!), you'll be glad you took the time to recalibrate.

Own the Career You're Building

I'll tell you the truth you won't often hear: When you step off the traditional path, you also step out of the safety net of external validation.

Like I alluded to earlier in the chapter, no one's handing out promotions for "Most Courageous Pivot." There's no LinkedIn badge for "Built Three Revenue Streams and Still Had Time for a Nap." You don't get gold stars for managing your energy or walking away from misaligned work—which means that the metrics you use, and the story you tell, is all on you.

Portfolio careerists don't really have a template to follow. We have to build the blueprint as we go.

Some days, that will feel powerful. Like you cracked the mysterious code. Other days, you'll wonder if everyone else got a copy of the instructions and you missed the memo. You'll find yourself second-guessing the quiet days, the strange projects, the path that looks nothing like your peers', and you'll wonder if you've veered off course.

Let me save you the spiral: You haven't.

You are on *your own course*. You are building a career that fits you, not one that always fits nicely into a dropdown menu. That takes guts! And it takes practice to accept it. Because when no one is telling you what the next step is, you have to learn to listen inward instead of always looking outward. That's the real work.

Owning your career means:

- Checking *your* metrics, not theirs.
- Honoring your energy, not just hustling for the sake of it.
- Saying no to good things to make room for the *right* things.
- Letting your career and goals evolve as you go.

Mini Career Manifesto: Define What You're Building

You've made it through the chaos, the strategy, the systems, and the energy checks—time to define what it all adds up.

Use the sentence below to distill and put words to the career you're building:

I'm building a career defined by _____, fueled by _____, and aligned with what matters most to me: _____.

Examples

- I'm building a career defined by *creative freedom*, fueled by *curiosity*, and aligned with what matters most to me: *real impact over empty titles*.

- I'm building a career defined by *autonomy*, fueled by *deep work*, and aligned with what matters most to me: *time with my family and work I'm proud of*.

- I'm building a career defined by *storytelling*, fueled by *strategy*, and aligned with matters most to me: *integrity and finding my community*.

Here's mine: I'm building a career defined by *autonomy* and *ownership*, fueled by *creativity and the desire to up-level and be better than I was yesterday*, and aligned with what matters most to me: *financial freedom, doing meaningful work with good people, and joy.*

Write it down, stick it on your wall, add it to your Notes app. Tattoo it on your forearm (okay, maybe not that far—but also, no judgment). This is your anchor. And when things feel wobbly (which they will!), zoom out. Look at the arc you're building. The values shaping your choices. Revisit your "why." Rebalance your buckets. And keep going. You're not behind, late, or lost. You're just doing something that a lot of people are too afraid to try: *building a career that actually fits.*

And that's rare. It's powerful. And it's yours. You don't need outside permission to build a career that is meaningful and sustainable. You just need to remember who's writing the story.

(Hint: It's you.)

Takeaways

- A portfolio career doesn't always come with milestones laid out in neat little steps. You're building the blueprint as you go. All of your wins, pivots, and quiet seasons count because they're part of a career that actually fits you.
- Flexibility is one of the biggest perks of a portfolio career, but without a little structure, it can spiral into chaos really fast. Creating frameworks that reflect your capacity, priorities, and working style will make sure your career stays sustainable and aligned.
- Protecting your time, energy, and focus is just as important as chasing opportunities. This type of work requires stamina. And you don't have to do it all. You must do what matters, consistently.

Building a Purposeful Portfolio Career

Chapter 7

Designing a Career That Grows with You

My father-in-law started working at a printing company in his late teens. He's worked there for more than 40 years, and he'll retire from that company in only a few short years. I admire him greatly for it.

But for the vast majority of the following generations, the world doesn't give us the chance to work that way anymore. Industries shift overnight, AI is turning entire fields upside down, and the tumultuous job market and economy have toppled even the most reliable companies. *The old blueprint is no longer a guarantee.*

If you're reading this, I'm guessing you already know that. You might even be living it. Maybe you've watched your industry transform in real time. Or perhaps you've realized that the linear path isn't for you and that your interests and goals shift every few years. Whatever brought you here, you're looking for something different: perhaps a career that's resilient in the face of change *and* flexible enough to accommodate your growth and evolving interests.

Spoiler alert: It's entirely possible, if you build it right.

Redefining Career Success

If the last few years have taught as anything, it's that stability can be an illusion. Instead of clinging to an old definition of "success," is it time to rethink what it means to "make it"?

A resilient, flexible career doesn't have to be about locking into one role for decades. It can be about

- developing adaptable skills,
- learning how to pivot when necessary, and
- building relationships that open new doors.

A friend of mine, Michelle, was a creative director at an ad agency for nearly a decade. Then, within a month, the agency lost two of its biggest clients. And within weeks, she was laid off, along with half of her team.

For months, she struggled. She had spent so long climbing the agency ladder that she hadn't built a backup plan—and at the time, a lot of agencies were reducing headcount. So rather than trying to force her way back into the same industry, she reevaluated what she actually wanted. She started freelancing, experimenting with different projects and clients. Within a year, she had tripled her old salary by consulting for multiple startups. Her resilience was no longer tied to a single paycheck. Instead, it stemmed from her ability to adapt.

This is the new career model: one that gives you control over your trajectory, no matter what's happening in the job market or economy.

Let's play out a hypothetical. If your entire industry collapsed tomorrow, would you still have marketable skills? If AI took over your job description, would you still bring something valuable and impactful to the table?

These questions aren't meant to send you in a spiral (I promise). But they're worth asking because change is inevitable. What's optional is whether you're prepared for it. As you build a flexible, resilient career, the objective should not be to dodge disruption. The objective is to make peace with the fact that it's part of the deal, then building a skill set that can outlast the chaos.

The Shift from Job Security to Skill Security

One of the biggest misconceptions about career resilience is that it's *all* about job security: finding a stable company, negotiating a solid salary, and hoping you'll be set. But real security comes from *skill* security: knowing that no matter where you work, what industry you're in, or how technology evolves, you bring something to the table that will always be valuable.

That kind of security doesn't live in a company org chart. It lives in your ability to think critically, solve problems, lead people, communicate clearly, and adapt when the ground shifts under your feet. Your skills aren't locked into one job or sector—but travel with you, grow with you, and open new doors when others close.

Instead of viewing shifts in your industry or career as threats, you can design your career in a way that embraces change as just part of the process. And instead of relying on external stability, we can future-proof our careers by strengthening some skills that will always be in demand.

Identify and Develop Adaptable Skills

Some skills go out of style fast. Others are timeless and can be applied across multiple industries and roles. The key is figuring out which of yours are built to last and which ones might need a refresh.

Take stock of your top five skills and ask yourself three questions:

1. Can I apply these skills across different roles or industries?

2. Are there skills I need to update or replace?

3. How can I strengthen my most transferable abilities?

See the following box to see how I would answer these questions.

Designing a Career That Grows with You

How I'd Answer These Questions

Top three to five skills (in no particular order):

1. Writing
2. Brand strategy
3. Public speaking and facilitation
4. Influencer and partnership strategy
5. Creative direction and content development

Can I apply these skills across different roles or industries?
Absolutely. Every industry needs clear, compelling communication. Whether I'm writing a keynote, scripting video ads, or helping a startup define their brand voice, the container might shift, but the core skills are versatile.

Are there skills I need to update or replace?
I used to lean heavily on social media management and execution (like scheduling posts, community engagement and management, etc.), but now I focus more on the *why* and *how*. That shift has freed me up to focus on different work and partner with folks who love the day-to-day. But it would probably be a good idea to maintain my skill set in social media management as a backup.

How can I strengthen my most transferable abilities?
Writing is a muscle, so I treat it like one. I write daily—for my newsletter, LinkedIn posts, or even in messy docs no one else will see. I also study great writing in all formats. And I ask for feedback often, from people I trust.

This is your roadmap. If you identify a skill that consistently shows up in your past roles and future interests (like storytelling, strategic thinking, leadership, etc.), double down on it. Invest in sharpening that edge. Take a course, ask for feedback, teach it to someone else, whatever helps you turn that skill into your calling card.

On the flip side, though, if you notice a skill that feels outdated or irrelevant to the direction you're heading, take it as feedback. This is your cue to let go, reframe, or upgrade. Maybe that means swapping "basic social media knowledge" with "platform-specific strategy" or replacing "good communicator" for "compelling presenter." You do not have to become good at everything. What we want to do here is become *known* for a few powerful, portable skills that make you a valuable asset, no matter what title, client, or industry is on the table.

Connect the Dots with a Throughline

You've done a lot. Maybe too much to fit neatly into a single job title. But identifying your stronger, most adaptable skills is the first half of the battle. The other half is learning how to communicate them in a way that makes people *get* it. And even if your path has zigzagged, that doesn't mean your career has been random. If anything, it's proof of your adaptability, curiosity, and ability to grow.

Chances are, there's been a *throughline* all along—a pattern, a perspective, a set of strengths you've carried from job to job, client to client, industry to industry. You just need a way to tell that story clearly, confidently, and in a way that clicks for clients, hiring managers, and potential collaborators.

The truth is that most people won't connect the dots for you. Because if *you* don't recognize the thread, how can you expect anyone else to? So, it's your job to give your career a narrative, or a lens that shows how it all fits together. *That* is your throughline.

Let's build it.

Career Throughline Builder

This exercise will help you connect the dots between different roles and experiences, so you can clearly articulate how your background makes you valuable. The objective is to shift from "I've had a bunch of unrelated jobs and industry pivots" to "Here's how my experience ties together."

Step 1: List out your key career chapters. Write down three to five pivotal roles, projects, or chapters from your work life. For each one, jot down the following:

- What you did.

- What you learned.

- What you loved (or hated).

- What results you achieved.

- *Bonus:* Think about the challenges you solved, the industry you navigated, and the results you achieved.

Example

Freelance Copywriter

- Wrote website and ad copy for tech startups
- Learned to write conversion-focused copy quickly, clearly, and effectively
- Loved the creative problem-solving and obscure, high-level problems
- Helped increase conversions by 20%+

Step 2: Spot the patterns. Now look at what you wrote. What themes show up across the board? There's likely a pattern or two.

Maybe you've always been the strategist in every role. Or maybe you're great at managing people, building relationships, and simplifying complex ideas. Ask yourself:

- What kind of work do I keep gravitating toward?
- What problems am I consistently solving?
- What skills or strengths pop up again and again?

Step 3: Write your 2-3 sentence narrative. This is your go-to pitch. Keep it clear, compelling, and not fluffy. Highlight the common thread(s) and focus on leading with value.

Bonus: You can use this for your website, bio, interviews, or those "Tell me about yourself" moments.

Formula to try: "I've built my career around [core strength or interest] and used that to [result or impact across roles]. My ability to [specific skill or perspective] ties together each and every chapter, from [early role] to [most recent one]."

Step 4: Say it out loud. Yes, literally. Record yourself explaining your career story. Try to keep it under 90 seconds. Does it sound cohesive? Do you feel proud of it? If not, tweak it until you do. And make sure to lead with the impact you create, not just with job titles.

Example

I've built my career around understanding human behavior and using that skill set to build strong, scalable marketing programs. My ability to adapt across industries makes me uniquely positioned to build strong brands and help businesses connect with their audiences.

Develop the Mindset of a Lifelong Learner

With this kind of career journey, standing still isn't an option. Skills evolve, industries shift, and what worked last week might feel outdated by tomorrow morning. Embracing the mindset of a lifelong learner means that you stay curious and adaptable. It doesn't mean you have to constantly chase the next credential or certification.

Think about the people in your field who always seem to stay ahead of the curve. I've met some folks like this over the years, and they're not necessarily the ones with the most traditional experience. But they *are* the ones who see learning as an ongoing process, whether it's picking up new skills, tackling emerging trends, or even rethinking old assumptions.

At one of my first marketing jobs, I worked with someone who had been in marketing for more than 20 years. She had deep industry knowledge, but she was still resisting social media. "I don't do social," she'd say in meetings. "I'll stick to what I know." And within a few years, her expertise had become a little less relevant. She was talented, but she refused to evolve.

On the flip side, another colleague took the opposite approach. He immersed himself in new platforms and leveraged his existing strengths to adapt rather than resist. The difference was pretty straightforward: One person saw learning as an inconvenience. The other saw it as an opportunity.

Adopting a learning mindset is one of the most powerful ways to approach your career. And honestly, your life. It allows you to shift gears without feeling like you're starting over because every new skill, experience, and perspective you gain builds on what's already there.

The Two Key Ingredients for a Career That Lasts: Resilience and Flexibility

There's a myth that if you just work hard enough, get the right degree, or follow the right checklist, your career will naturally fall into place. But anyone who's built a career in the past decade, especially outside the confines of a single corporate ladder, knows that longevity takes more than hustle. It takes resilience and flexibility. They're the unsung superpowers of every portfolio careerist, entrepreneur, and multi-hyphenate out there building something that doesn't fit neatly into a box.

I've had seasons where I went from leading marketing at a startup to scaling my business, hosting a podcast, and writing a book. The only reason it worked is because I knew how to bend without breaking.

Resilience is what keeps you going when things get weird (which they will). I once heard it described as being able to stay present even while the world, or your circumstances, feel like too much. And *flexibility* is what helps you change direction *without* losing momentum.

Together, they make your career sustainable and, honestly, survivable. Because the fact of the matter is, the market will change. Clients will ghost. Your role will evolve. Industries will pivot. You can't control the chaos, but you can build a mindset and model that rolls with it.

Resilience: Embracing the Swim

I used to hear the word *resilient* and think of someone stoic, bulletproof, and *blissfully* unbothered by life's curveballs. But as much as resilience is about enduring hardship, it's also about transforming challenges into opportunities. You don't have to be unshakable because resilience is about being rebuildable. It's knowing you might get knocked sideways and still trusting your ability to come back stronger and clearer (and maybe even funnier).

Elfried Samba, cofounder and CEO of Butterfly Effect, a leading social media agency, knows this all too well. After leaving his role as Global Head of Social at Gymshark, Elfried dove headfirst into entrepreneurship, a shift he likens to swimming in the open ocean. "You never get closer, and every now and again, there are sharks in the water. The solution is to fall in love with swimming because it never ends," he explains.

His journey from the stability of corporate life to the uncertainty of running his own business wasn't easy. He described the transition as going from a world where "everything was predictable—you have a house, a nice car, a steady salary—to what I call freefall." But what kept him going was embracing the discomfort.

Resilience is about enduring the hard parts, yes, but it's also about falling in love with the process, no matter how unpredictable it may be. "Entrepreneurship is a game of who can hang on the longest," Elfried told me. "It's about showing up consistently and embracing the journey."[1]

You need to be able to stay grounded, even when your external reality shakes. It's emotional endurance. Mental agility. And the belief that, even if you're in a tough spot, you've figured things out before, and you can do it again. So how do you even build that kind of resilience?

How to Build Career Resilience in a Real, Human Way

Develop your "bounce back" ritual. One thing we're not going to do is fall into toxic positivity. I'm talking about real, concrete actions that help you process a setback so that you don't get stuck in it. It could be walking your dog, listening to a podcast, or even just voice-noting your best friend to say, "Okay, I'm spiraling. Talk me off the ledge." For me, it usually entails stepping away from my screen, doing something active (lifting weights, bouldering, a barre class), and forcing myself to get my mind off it and out of reactive mode. You need rituals that remind you you're safe, capable, and still in control, even when circumstances feel shaky.

Detach your worth from your wins. Brutal but necessary. When your self-worth is tied to your last client project or your current revenue stream, you'll *constantly* feel like you're failing the minute things slow down. A healthy sense of self has to live outside of your job title, your next speaking gig, or your inbox. Otherwise, every "no" feels personal. Remember: You are not your deliverables. You're not your Q2 numbers. You are a full human being who happens to work; you are not a productivity machine.

Don't just ask, "Why is this happening to me?" Ask, "What is this teaching me?" This shift changed everything for me. It doesn't mean you can't be disappointed or annoyed when something doesn't go your way. But instead of letting that frustration fester, try turning it into a chance to grow or learn. What didn't work here? What will you do differently next time? The faster you can move from "This sucks" to "Here's what I learned," the faster you start rebuilding.

Have a short memory when it comes to missed opportunities. Athletes are taught to shake off a bad play quickly—not because it didn't matter, but because obsessing over it can cost them the next one. Same thing here. Learn from the mistake, take a beat, and then move forward. You cannot lead yourself (or your career) if you're dragging every misstep around with you.

Set your own damn milestones. You know what builds real confidence and resilience? Celebrating your own markers of progress, not just the big public ones. Did you finish a project that terrified you? Sent the pitch you've been scared to put out there? Maybe you protected your time this week and said no to something misaligned. Celebrate that. Don't wait for some imaginary gatekeeper to hand you a ribbon. Define your own markers of growth and recognize them when they happen.

Flexibility: The Underrated Professional Superpower

If resilience is the ability to handle adversity, then flexibility is the willingness to shape-shift in response. It allows you to adapt without losing your sense of direction. It's the skill of adjusting your approach without abandoning your goals. And when you're building a portfolio career—or honestly, just trying to stay levelheaded in such a rapidly evolving market and world—it's *everything*.

Now, let's be clear. Being flexible doesn't mean saying yes to *everything*. It doesn't mean you have to shape-shift for every client request or pivot so often that you don't know which way is up. But you can stay rooted in your strengths while remaining open to new opportunities and ideas.

Here's how I think about it: I say yes to the things that complement my core strengths. I say no to the things that drain me, dilute my focus, or make me want to run into the woods and never look back. For example, I've built my brand and reputation around influencer marketing, content, and growth marketing. I don't do PR. I no longer shoot photography or manage video production. Not because I can't, but because I don't *want* to.

By being strategic and flexible, I'm able to shift my focus when the market shifts, or when I shift, without scrapping everything I've built. I can pause one part of my business to double down on another, and everything still fits. And it can be the same for you. You can build a diversified portfolio that still feels cohesive, instead of stretching yourself too thin across a dozen unrelated skill sets.

The result: consistent, engaging work, and a career that can weather anything.

Balancing Your Personal and Professional Growth

It's easy to see your career as completely separate from your personal life, as if you're two entirely different people: "work" you and "real" you. (Maybe *Severance*, the Apple TV+ series, was onto something.) And while it's crucial to have boundaries between the two, both sides influence each other constantly. When you're personally fulfilled, you're bound to be more confident, creative, and resilient at work. And when your career challenges you (in a good way), it can spark personal growth.

But real balance is more than squeezing self-care or trying to "leave work at work." At its core, it's about designing a life where your career fuels you rather than drains you—and that starts with finding work-life harmony.

Morgan Ingram put it this way:

> I realized that I needed to figure out, "Who is Morgan? What do I enjoy? What excites me? What do I want to do outside of work?" I wanted to have things to talk about beyond just my job—to feel more well-rounded instead of just running on autopilot. I found that the times I feel the most fulfilled or excited are when I'm on an adventure. So, I had to ask myself, "How can I make *my life* feel like an adventure, with main quests and side quests?"[2]

The shift from defining yourself solely by work to seeing life as an evolving, multilayered experience can change everything. You can make sure your career doesn't become your identity, without checking out of your career. And you can give yourself permission to explore new interests, hobbies, and goals that make you a more well-rounded person.

For some, that might mean picking up a new language or sport, like Morgan's journey into learning Japanese and playing pickleball. For others, it might be prioritizing creative outlets, deepening friendships, or simply making more space for rest.

Whatever it is, it's a reminder that your career should complement your life, not consume it. That's not to say that there won't be seasons in our lives where we have to give more to work than our personal lives and vice versa. But professional growth without personal growth is unsustainable. You can't just focus on career goals and assume everything else will fall into place. The more you nurture your personal life, the more equipped you are to handle professional challenges, and the more fulfilling your career will be in the long run. That's how you keep it sustainable.

The Journey Never Ends (and That's a Good Thing!)

If you're waiting for the day where you can sit back and say, "Okay, I've made it! I can stop growing and evolving now!" ... Well, you might be waiting forever. A nontraditional career is a permanent work in progress. But that's an advantage, not a burden. It keeps you curious. It keeps you adaptable. It keeps you future proof.

The fear of change fades when you expect change. Over time, you realize that there is no final destination. There's just the next iteration of who you're becoming.

Takeaways

- Skill security is the new job security. You can't rely on a job title, employer, or industry to keep you safe, especially in a world that's evolving so fast. Focus on sharpening the skills that can travel with you across roles, sectors, and seasons.
- Your career path doesn't need to make traditional sense. It needs to make sense to *you*. The key is connecting the dots and owning the through line. Learn to articulate how your zigzags add up to something strategic, purposeful, and powerful.
- The ability to bounce back and shift gears is no longer just a "nice to have." It's how you build a career that lasts. When you blend resilience with flexibility, you stop chasing uncertainty and start building sustainably.

Designing a Career That Grows with You

Chapter 8

Avoiding Burnout

If there's one thing I've learned the hard way about being a portfolio careerist, it's this: Burnout doesn't discriminate. It will take you down. Fast.

Contrary to what you might believe (and what I used to think), diversification alone doesn't magically protect you from overwork, stress, or that creeping sense of fatigue that makes you want to throw your laptop out the nearest window (or is that just me?). In fact, juggling multiple clients, projects, and side ventures can lead to a unique flavor of burnout—one that sneaks up on you while you're busy thinking:

- *Well, at least this is better than being stuck in a 9-to-5.*
- *At least I'm doing what I love.*
- *Yeah, but at least I'm making good money.*

I hate to break it to you, but burnout doesn't care about your "at leasts." And it doesn't care if you're passionate about your work. I know this firsthand.

At one point in my mid-20s, I had three jobs at the same time:

- A full-time job at a pediatric therapy clinic (which became remote after a couple of months).

- A remote role at an events company (20 hours per week).

- A remote role for an e-commerce brand (20–30 hours per week).

For the first few months, I thought I was a productivity machine. My calendars were synced up and color-coded to perfection. The money was rolling in. Nothing could touch me. I was unstoppable! Then, around the six-month mark, things started to shift:

- I woke up feeling like I'd pulled all-nighters. Every day.

- No amount of sleep, exercise, or ice water helped.

- By 10 a.m., I was running on fumes.

- Everything felt overwhelming. Even a 15-minute Zoom call seemed unbearable.

Initially, I convinced myself I was just physically exhausted. And yes, that was part of it, but the exhaustion ran deeper than that. I was emotionally and mentally tapped out. The enthusiasm I once had for my work was gone. My brain was constantly foggy. I was losing patience over minor things.

In hindsight, the warning signs were there all along. But I ignored them because I thought I could outwork burnout.

Spoiler alert: I couldn't. And neither can you.

What Is Burnout? (It's More Than Just Exhaustion)

Burnout isn't just about feeling tired. It's a state of emotional, physical, and mental exhaustion caused by prolonged stress. According to the World Health Organization (WHO), burnout is defined by three dimensions:

- Energy depletion or exhaustion (You wake up already drained.)

- Increased mental distance from your job (You start resenting everything about your job.)
- Reduced professional efficacy (You feel like no matter how much you work, nothing is getting done.)[1]

Basically, your brain and body are screaming, "Enough already!"

The good news is that burnout doesn't have to be inevitable. You can build a career (and life) that won't crumble under the weight of a thousand to-dos and your own expectations.

If you don't build safeguards into your work life, burnout will come for you. Let's stop that from happening.

Rebuild the Rules Before Burnout Builds a Home

Before we talk about task batching, boundaries, or the magic of saying "no," we need to address something deeper: the internal operating system that got you here. There's a common misconception that burnout just comes from doing too much. But really, it comes from doing too much of the wrong things in a way that doesn't work for you, driven by expectations you never actually agreed to or align with.

We don't burn out because we're weak. We burn out because we've been conditioned to believe that saying "yes" is what makes us, and our work, valuable. That rest is earned. That slowing down means falling behind. And a lot of us are burnt out because we're chasing someone else's definition of success—one we never stopped to question. Maybe it's a version of success you built years ago when you thought "making it" meant long hours, a fancy title, and a company car. Maybe it's the version you inherited from parents, mentors, or social media, convincing you that if you're not exhausted, you're not trying hard enough.

These beliefs—often outdated, inherited, or fed by the algorithm—are the invisible architecture of burnout.

And so, without ever realizing it, you start operating under rules you never agreed to:

- *I have to triple my income in six months, by any means necessary.*
- *I can't afford to take breaks.*
- *Saying no means I'm lazy.*

You start playing a game where burnout is inevitable. And expected. The worst part, though, is that when you hit that wall—when you wake up feeling like your body and brain are on strike—you don't take it as a sign that something is broken. You take it as proof that you're not working hard enough.

This is the trap. This is how burnout wins. And you're basically handing burnout a VIP invite into your life.

Unlearn the Old Script

We've all heard it before: *Work hard enough and success will follow. Grind now, shine later. Sleep when you're dead.*

Catchy slogans, I guess. Terrible in practice and a one-way ticket to burnout. The old ambition script tells us that if we're not drowning in output, we're not trying hard enough. If we're not exhausted, then that must mean we're not ambitious. And the wildest part is that it *works* for a while. You grind. You get the dopamine hits, the client referrals, the promotions. Until one day, you realize that you're building someone else's dream or vision of success. And slowly losing yourself in the process.

So how do we rewrite the script?

Rewrite your ambition from the inside out. Start with your effort-to-impact ratio. Where is your energy and focus actually making a difference, and where are they just making you *look* productive? Not every idea needs to be a new project. Not every project deserves your immediate attention. Take inventory of what's really driving progress in your career and start ruthlessly editing the rest. Just because you *can* do something doesn't mean it deserves your energy.

Audit your goals like you audit your finances. Ask yourself, "Am I doing this because it lights me up or because it makes me *look* impressive? Am I pursuing this opportunity because it aligns with my goals or because someone I admire said I should *want* this?" Ambition without self-awareness is a trap. And if you don't question the "why" behind your goals, you might wake up five years from now wondering why all of your wins feel empty.

Let rest be proof of progress. If you can't take a full day off without feeling like you need to justify it to the ghost of capitalism, then you have a problem. Your worth isn't defined by your output. Rest is productive. Play is powerful. And a quiet season means you're human—it doesn't mean that you're slacking.

Try this: Spend a weekend doing *nothing* that scales. No "catching up on work." No "just one quick email." Let yourself be a person, not a brand. See how you feel on Monday. The reality is that ambition isn't the enemy. But the version we inherited is outdated and broken. And you don't need to burn yourself down to build something valuable.

What you need is a new framework that prioritizes clarity over chaos, intention over ego, and energy over aesthetics. You need a framework that actually lets you enjoy what you're building, instead of just surviving it.

Find Clarity

You could be the most talented, driven, unstoppable person in the world. But if you're not clear on what actually matters, what's worth your energy, and what you're building toward, then it's all just noise. You'll be overcommitted, under-stimulated, and under-fulfilled.

You'll say yes to everything because you haven't figured out what deserves a no.

Elfried Samba described this beautifully: "It's a fusion between art and science. You need the energy to drive your creativity and the clarity to channel it into something meaningful. Without that balance, you're just spinning your wheels."[2]

Look, I've been there. I've had the 12-tab chaos. I've started a day with six different priorities and ended it wondering how I somehow got none of them done. When you're juggling multiple projects, clients, or responsibilities, the default is to move faster. But speed without clarity won't solve anything.

So, what can you do?

- *Audit your efforts.* What is actually generating results for you, emotionally, financially, or creatively? Do more of that.

- *Name your season.* Are you in a building season? A coasting season? A scaling season? You can't evaluate your output if you haven't defined the purpose behind it.

- *Create a focus filter.* Before you say yes to anything, ask your-self: Does this align with what I say I care about? If not, why am I entertaining it?

Clarity is about alignment, not about perfection. You don't need a five-year plan if you don't feel ready for one. You just need to stop saying yes to things that drag you out of alignment with your values, energy, or goals.

Now, let's talk about the other piece of the puzzle: community.

Surround Yourself with a Supportive Community

You might think your work is a solo sport. It's not. In fact, burnout thrives in isolation. One of the most overlooked tools for burnout prevention is having people around you who remind you that you're more than just your work.

Elfried put it simply: "Sometimes you need people around you who help you disconnect, who remind you that there's more to your life than just work."[3]

And it's true. When you're surrounded by people who normalize the nonstop hustle, at any cost, you might start to think it's the only way. But when you build community with people who prioritize wholeness over just busyness—who check in on *you*, not just your wins—it becomes easier to zoom out. To rest. To breathe. To work hard and hustle when you need to, but always recognize the value of breaks and rest.

Whether it's a group chat, a coworker, a mentor, or a partner who closes your laptop for you when it's time to rest, burnout has a harder time creeping in when you're not alone with your spinning thoughts. So yes, build the systems. Set the boundaries. But also, find your people. The ones who see the *full* version of you, not just the highlight reel. Clarity without connection is still not sustainable.

And in case no one's said it lately, you're allowed to be ambitious *and* supportive. Strategic *and* soft. Focused *and* human. That's how you build something that lasts.

How to Stay in the Game Without Burning Out

When your career is built on a portfolio of clients, projects, and commitments, burnout can feel like it's built into the model. But it doesn't have to be! One thing I had to learn was that I didn't have to spend my career bouncing between exhaustion and recovery. But you have to be willing to play the long game: building a system that keeps you sharp, focused, and fully in control of your workload.

This is how you do it.

Learn the Art of Saying No (Without the Guilt)

If you're constantly overcommitting, overextending, and overexplaining, you're on the fast track to burnout. Saying "yes" to everything might feel like the right move at first, since it typically leads to more opportunities, more clients, and more income, but all it does is dilute your focus and energy.

Instead of asking, "Should I do this?" ask yourself, "What am I giving up if I say yes to this?"

Every "yes" has a hidden cost. Maybe it's time with your family. Maybe it's the ability to take on a higher-value project later.

The Fix: Use the "Hell Yes" Filter

Sometimes you have to take on a project or initiative because it's required. But in situations where the choice is up to you, use the framework in Table 6.1 to decide what deserves your time.

Pro Tip: If saying "no" feels awkward, try these responses:

- I appreciate the opportunity, but I don't have the bandwidth to give this the attention it deserves.

- This isn't the right fit for me, but I'd love to stay connected for future opportunities.

You don't have to close a door forever when you say "no." You can keep the right doors open, even if now isn't the right time.

Table 6.1 Hell Yes Filter

Question	If the Answer Is "No" ...
Does this align with my goals?	Decline it. Focus on what does.
Am I excited to do this?	If it's not a "hell yes," it's probably a no.
Is this the best use of my energy and time?	Prioritize work that moves the needle.
Will this add unnecessary stress?	Protect your peace. Decline.

Stop Letting Context Switching Kill Your Focus

It's one thing to have a single boss expecting your full attention. But a portfolio career can mean juggling half a dozen "bosses" at once, each with their own deadlines, priorities, and demands on your time.

On the one hand, it sounds like the dream, right? You set your own schedule, work on exciting things, and get to avoid the monotony you might feel in a traditional job. But what no one tells you is how mentally exhausting it can be to constantly switch gears. One moment, you're in deep creative work, fully locked in. The next, you're hopping on a Zoom call for a completely different project. Then, just as you start making progress on an important project, your inbox pings with an "urgent" request, throwing you off track.

This constant *context switching*—jumping from one task or mindset to another—can be a silent productivity killer. The problem is that your brain isn't just "switching tasks" like it's no big deal; it's resetting entirely each time. Think of it like closing and reopening a dozen browser tabs all day long. It drains your energy, slows you down, and makes even simple tasks feel harder than they should.

And if you're not careful, it can lead to the kind of exhaustion that makes you question if you're actually good at *anything*, when the reality is that you're just not giving yourself enough focus time to do great work.

So how do we nip this in the bud?

The Fix: Task Batching

Instead of bouncing between different kinds of tasks all day, try batching similar work together. Morgan told me how he structures his days with intention to minimize distractions and maximize focus. Rather than letting his schedule dictate his focus, he takes control by theming his days.

Mondays are for internal meetings and one-to-ones, Tuesdays are stacked with sales calls, and Wednesdays, his "Maker Days", are completely off-limits.

"Wednesday is my favorite day," he told me. "No meetings, no distractions. Don't talk to me. Don't hit me up. Don't send me a voice note. It's deep work from 5:30 a.m. to 3:00 p.m. I'm locked in, getting stuff done."

By blocking his time this way, he's minimizing the mental friction of jumping between unrelated tasks. And instead of scattering meetings and deep work throughout his week, he's created a structure that allows him to be fully present in whatever mode he's in, whether that's problem-solving with his team, closing deals, or producing high-quality content.

How I Do It: The Color-coded Calendar System

Morgan batches his work by day, but I operate with a hybrid task-batching/themed workday model. I color-code my calendar and batch tasks by the hour or time frame, so I can visually see how my time is allocated at a glance and carve out space for what matters most.

My categories include the following:

- Speaking Engagements
- Focus Time and Deep Work
- External Meetings and Events
- Client Calls
- Content and Podcast Work
- Client Discovery Calls
- Personal Commitments
- Buffer Blocks
- Meetings *for* My Business

I set hard rules for my availability:

- No calls on Mondays (so I don't start off my week in reaction mode)
- Limited calls on Fridays (to wind down the week instead of cramming it with last-minute meetings)
- Wednesdays = Deep Work Day (a full day blocked off for execution)

If you talk to any of my friends or close family, I guarantee they'll all say the same thing: I live by my calendar. (*I like to joke that if it's not on my calendar, it doesn't exist.*) This structure helps me balance different priorities without feeling pulled in a million directions. And it works for me because it provides structure without feeling rigid. Some weeks, I need more focus time. Others, I might have more speaking engagements and client meetings. But it's easy to shift things around while still protecting my time.

Find What Works for You

I'm not telling you to copy exactly what Morgan or I do. It's up to you to find a structure that fits your workflow, energy levels, and commitments. Some people thrive on themed workdays. Others prefer color-coded time blocks. Some prefer something else altogether.

Our goal here is to reduce unnecessary context switching so you're not constantly draining mental energy trying to switch between different modes of work.

Take time to identify your ideal work rhythm. Ask yourself:

- When do I do my best deep work? Morning, afternoon, or evening?
- Which tasks drain me the most?
- How can I group similar tasks together?
- What times of day am I naturally more focused? Block these for deep work.
- When do I feel most social and engaged? Do your best to schedule calls and meetings then.

At the end of the day, context switching is not so much a productivity issue as it is an energy issue. If you feel drained before you've even gotten through half your to-do list, your work won't be sustainable.

By structuring your time intentionally, you give your brain the space to actually do its best work. And that's how you build a career that's both fulfilling *and* effective.

Build a Self-care System That Actually Works

I hate to say it, but burnout isn't solved with a bubble bath. Real self-care is necessary for career maintenance. It's not just about indulgence.

If you're not taking care of your mind, body, and emotions, everything else starts to fall apart. And no, this doesn't mean you have to overhaul your entire life overnight. But you can start building small habits that keep you from hitting a breaking point.

The Fix: Prioritize Self-care (Without Making It a Full-time Job)

Self-care gets thrown around like a universal prescription. *Take a bath. Light a candle. Go for a walk.* But if you're just checking boxes because someone on the internet told you to, it's not self-care. It's obligation in disguise.

The point is to figure out what actually helps you feel good, reset, and function like a whole human being instead of a burnt-out shell. Here's how to do that.

- *Pay attention to what fuels versus drains you.* Think of your energy like a budget. Every task, meeting, or project is either a withdrawal or a deposit. If you're constantly in the red, you're setting yourself up for burnout. The goal is to spend your energy where it matters and protect it from unnecessary drains.

Energy Audit: Where Are You Draining Yourself?

At the end of each week, take inventory of what's fueling you versus what's draining you:

Task/Project	How did this make me feel?	Did this add or drain energy?
_____	Energized / Neutral / Drained	Adds energy / Drains energy
_____	Energized / Neutral / Drained	Adds energy / Drains energy
_____	Energized / Neutral / Drained	Adds energy / Drains energy

(continued)

Avoiding Burnout

(continued)

Use this audit to answer the following questions for yourself:

- What gave me energy today?
- What drained me?
- What did I do because I *thought* I should, not because I actually wanted to?

Patterns will start to emerge. Maybe meetings before 9 a.m. aren't as productive, but deep work in the morning gives you momentum. Or maybe certain tasks and clients drain you more than they should. Sometimes, the answers surprise you. You might think you need total solitude to charge, but then realize a low-key dinner with close friends actually lifts you up. Maybe you assume self-care = stillness, but you feel better after movement. The key is to observe, *not* assume.

Pro Tip: Design your work around your energy, not just your hours. The more intentional you can be about when and how you work, the more sustainable everything will feel (and be).

- *Know the difference between numbing and recharging.* Not everything that *feels* like relief is actually rest. When you're exhausted, it's easy to fall into habits that numb you—zoning out in front of a screen, mindlessly scrolling, and so on. And sure, these things might help you disconnect, but do they actually restore you?

  Here's the difference: *Numbing out* is passive. It makes time disappear. But you're not engaged; you're just escaping. And when you're done, you don't feel better. You feel foggier, heavier, or more drained. *Recharging* is intentional. It fills your energy reserves. You come out of it feeling clearer, lighter, or more grounded.

The test is if you feel worse afterward. If you feel more exhausted, more irritable, or like you wasted time, it wasn't self-care. It was avoidance. Next time you're reaching for a distraction, pause and ask, *Will this actually help me recharge or just make me forget I'm tired for a little while?*

Self-care is about creating the kind of rest that actually restores you, not about numbing yourself to exhaustion.

- *Experiment, then track what actually works.* Finding what energizes you is a process. It doesn't have to be a one-and-done decision.

Try this: Pick one *small* habit to test for two weeks. Maybe it's a 10-minute walk after work or putting your phone down 30 minutes before bed. Or maybe it's a "joy break" where you do something just for fun. At the end of each week, check in with yourself:

- Did this actually make me feel better?

- Was it easy to stick with?

- Do I *want* to keep doing it?

If it works, keep it. If it doesn't, put it to the side and try something else. The goal is to build something that *fits* your life.

- *Design a system that works* with *your life (not against it).* People often fail at self-care because they think it has to be a *huge* lifestyle overhaul. It doesn't. Ask yourself:

- *When do I naturally have energy?* Schedule self-care around *that*, not when you're already running on fumes.

- *What would make my day easier?* A better morning routine? A real lunch break? A hard stop on meetings after 5 p.m.?

- *What do I always wish I had more time for?* Make space for it before life fills that space.

Practicing self-care is a balancing act between adding new things and removing what drains you. So, if something is stealing your time, sapping your energy, or compromising your health, cut it loose.

What This Looks Like for Me

I don't have some rigid, perfectly optimized routine, but I *do* have self-care habits that work for me:

- *Therapy:* Therapy keeps me grounded, helps me process stress, and gives me space to work through challenges before they snowball.

- *Carving out time for my favorite hobbies:* Analyzing movies and reading are fun for me, but they're also a creative reset. I protect that time.

- *Exercise I actually enjoy:* I lift four times a week and do Pilates or Barre on the other days. If I hate it, I won't do it, so I make sure it's something I *want* to show up for.

- *A set bedtime (yes, really):* I protect my sleep like it's an important meeting. Because it kind of is.

- *Intentional rest:* Sometimes that means meditation, journaling, or, yes, a bubble bath. Self-care has to be more than a bunch of "treat yourself" moments, but those moments can (and should) be part of it.

Takeaways

- Burnout thrives in misalignment, not just overwork. If your goals, habits, or systems no longer reflect what actually matters to you, burnout will sneak in through the cracks.
- Preventing burnout is about building a work rhythm that protects your energy, honors your focus, and adapts to your reality. Learn how to say no without guilt, reduce context switching, and design a schedule around what energizes you.
- You don't have to do it alone. Make sure you're building relationships that anchor you to your full identity, not just your output.

Chapter 9

Holding Focus in a Multi-passionate Career

I'll never forget the day I had a full-blown existential crisis while chopping peppers.

I was standing in my kitchen, making lunch and emailing a client, while mentally preparing for a podcast interview that was happening in less than an hour. I still had to submit a marketing proposal by end of day, build a social media calendar for a client, and watch and review 10 films for a local film festival in the next three days.

If I were a computer, I'd have had about 97,000 tabs open. My brain was spinning, my laptop wouldn't stop dinging, and I was beginning to think I had no idea what I was doing with my life. Or with those peppers.

At first, I convinced myself that everything was okay (*Ha!*). But when my partner walked in, took one look at me, and asked if I was okay, my smile cracked.

I didn't hate the work. I loved all of it. But that was the problem. I wasn't burning out because I was directionless. I was burning out because I was trying to give *everything* equal urgency, priority, and energy. I had no plan and no structure, just vibes (and not the good kind).

I didn't want to pick one thing. I didn't want to simplify my career into one neat job title. But I also couldn't keep sprinting through every week like I was auditioning for *America's Next Top Burnout*.

That's the part people miss when they say, "You can do anything, just not *everything*" or "You can't do/have it all." They make it sound like you have to pick just *one* thing and drop everything else. Like the only answer is to shrink yourself. But it's not. The real answer is to be intentional about *how* you hold it all. And that starts with knowing how you work best, so you can build a structure that truly works for *you*.

Know Your Multi-hyphenate Work Style

You've probably heard the term *multi-hyphenate* before. It's a slightly fancy way of saying, "I do a lot of things, thanks for asking." Think actor-director-writer. Or entrepreneur-investor-creator-strategist-podcast-host-with-a-Substack.

Basically, if your résumé reads like a menu and you regularly get asked, "Wait … so what do you do exactly?" you're probably a multi-hyphenate.

Before you can build a structure that supports your multifaceted career, you need to understand how you actually work. Not how you think you *should* work. Not how your favorite productivity or corporate influencer works. How *you* work. Not all multi-hyphenates operate the same way. Some of us deep dive into one project at a time, then switch. Others thrive on juggling multiple projects at once. Some cycle through creative seasons. Others keep everything running in parallel. None of these styles are wrong. But one (or a blend) is probably right for you.

And you don't have to pick just one either! Most people are a mix. Nothing says you have to box yourself in, but it helps to name your patterns so you can work with them, not against them. The more clearly you can identify and understand how your brain works, the easier it is to make smart, aligned decisions about what to take on, what to let go, and how to structure your days in a way that doesn't make you want to run into the woods.

So, let's break it down. The multi-hyphenate types we're about to walk through aren't designed to be overly rigid or strict. Use them to spot your patterns, name your strengths, and build a structure that supports the life and career you're trying to build.

The Sequential Multi-hyphenate

If you are a sequential multi-hyphenate, you go all in on one thing for months or years before shifting, like a startup founder who eventually transitions into investing.

Your work life is probably built on intense focus and deep dives. You commit to one thing at a time, master it, and then pivot when you're ready for the next challenge. You might spend five years as a designer before deciding to go full-time into writing. Or launch a business, scale it, sell it, and then start over in a completely new industry.

It's not the same as abandoning old passions or interests. You just cycle through them in big, intentional chunks.

Your Biggest Challenge	What Helps
Feeling guilty for moving on when people expect you to "stick with it"	Give yourself permission to pivot with purpose. Set clear exit points or milestones so you know when it's time to shift gears.

The Cyclical Multi-hyphenate

If you are a cyclical multi-hyphenate, you rotate between multiple interests regularly, keeping them all active in some capacity—like someone who freelances in marketing, sells art on the side, and picks up a new skill every quarter. Your brain thrives on variety.

Sticking to one thing for too long feels stagnant, and you work best when you can switch between different projects.

Your Biggest Challenge	What Helps
Avoiding the feeling that you're constantly "starting over" or never making enough progress	Planned rotation points. Instead of shifting "randomly," build a schedule where each focus area gets its dedicated time so that nothing gets neglected.

The Parallel Multi-hyphenate

If you are a parallel multi-hyphenate, you run multiple careers or projects simultaneously at full capacity—like someone who works full-time in tech sales, runs an agency, and consults startups—all at the same time.

You *stack* instead of rotating. Your passions coexist rather than compete. Your life is built around balancing multiple things at once, and you like having different streams of work happening in parallel. Maybe you run a business, host a podcast, and create content at the same time. Or maybe you work a full-time job but also actively manage a side hustle and a creative project.

Your Biggest Challenge	What Helps
Overcommitting and stretching yourself too thin	Clear boundaries and prioritization. Not everything can be a top priority all the time!

The Seasonal Multi-hyphenate

If you are a seasonal multi-hyphenate, certain projects take precedence during specific months of the year, while others go dormant. I know a consultant who works as a wedding photographer during Arizona's prime wedding season, teaches online courses in the summer, and freelances in between.

You flow with the seasons, and your work naturally cycles based on external factors. You might have an intense work period followed by a quieter season where you experiment, rest, or shift focus.

Your Biggest Challenge	What Helps
Feeling pressure to be "productive" year-round, even when you know you need slower seasons	Embracing downtime as part of your success. Every season doesn't have to be about grinding. Some are for resetting, strategizing, and laying the groundwork for what's next.

What kind of multi-hyphenate am I? I'm a mix: primarily parallel, with a dash of sequential. My core work (running my business, consulting, speaking, and creating content) is always active, making me parallel at my foundation. But I also have sequential moments where I'll go all in on a big project (like writing this book) and temporarily deprioritize other things. Everything stays in motion, but the weight and priority shift depending on what's most important at the time.

Now, let's figure out which of these multi-hyphenate styles fits you best. Once you recognize how you naturally operate, you can stop fighting yourself and start working with your strengths.

Find Your Natural Work Style

Before you start building (or rebuilding) your career structure or work style, you have to understand how you naturally operate. And while I'm not trying to force you into a mold, the objective is to help you notice your own patterns so you can stop fighting them and start building a system that plays to your strengths.

Step 1: Reflect on how you naturally work

Ask yourself:

- Do I like going *all in* on something before switching gears? → You might be sequential.

- Do I need constant variety to stay engaged? → You might be cyclical.

- Do I want multiple things running at once without rotating them? → You might be parallel.

- Do my interests (or opportunities) naturally shift depending on the season? → You might be seasonal.

Remember, no style is better than the others!

Step 2: Look at your current projects

Now that you've got a sense of your natural work style, let's see if your workload actually reflects it or fights against it. In Table 9.1, you'll see some common alignments between your natural style and how your work is currently structured.

Spoiler alert: Like we talked about in a previous chapter, every day of work won't feel like a picnic in the park. But if *everything* feels hard *all the time*, it might be because you're setting yourself up to operate in a way that doesn't align with how you actually thrive.

Table 9.1 Aligning Natural Style and Work

If You're Naturally …	But You're Doing This …	Then It Makes Sense That You Feel …
Sequential	Juggling 10 active projects at once	Scattered, unfocused, constantly behind
Cyclical	Forcing yourself to pick one thing forever	Restless, creatively stuck, stagnant
Parallel	Trying to stagger everything into tidy "seasons"	Constrained, disorganized
Seasonal	Expecting consistent energy all year long	Burned out, uninspired

So, if you see yourself in one (or more) of these rows, that's your cue: it's time to recalibrate.

Step 3: Adjust your career to fit your natural flow

Let's take what you've learned and actually apply it. Table 9.2 is a breakdown of how each multi-hyphenate type might structure their work in a way that honors their energy, focus, and rhythm. Use these as starting points to help you rethink how you organize your time and attention.

Remember: Most people aren't just one thing. They're a mix. Maybe you're primarily parallel, but you go on full-on sequential mode when you're heads-down on a big project. Or you thrive in a cyclical rhythm nine months out of the year and then shift into seasonal flow when life calls for it. You've spent the whole book rejecting the idea of squeezing into a box or someone else's idea of success. Keep that same energy here.

Holding Focus in a Multi-passionate Career

Table 9.2 Structuring Work

Work Style	How to Structure Your Career
Sequential	Commit deeply to one or two projects at a time. Schedule built-in pivot points or sabbaticals to explore something new.
Cyclical	Set up regular "rotations": dedicated weeks or months for different interests and projects, while keeping all alive in some capacity.
Parallel	Stack two or three consistent streams of work. You might want to consider using tools or systems to streamline the juggling act and avoid being overwhelmed.
Seasonal	Lean into busy seasons with intention. But make sure you're building in lighter seasons for rest, creative exploration, or back-burner projects.

Once you've got a sense of your natural work style, you can use it as a compass, not a wrecking ball. You don't need to overhaul your entire life overnight. Start small. Take a look at your week: What can you shift to better reflect how you focus, what energizes you, or how you move through different kinds of work?

One shift. One edit. One tiny boundary can unlock way more clarity than a complete career detour. And once you get in the habit of noticing what works for you, and what doesn't, you can start building a life that isn't just full, but actually functional, and a career that feels like it fits.

Build a Structure That Actually Works (for You)

If you've made it this far in the chapter, you've started identifying your natural work style and have hopefully reframed your multi-hyphenate brain as a strength, not a liability. But recognizing your rhythm is just the beginning. Knowing you're a parallel operator or a seasonal sprinter doesn't do much if everything on your plate still feels equally urgent or if every idea feels like it needs to happen *right now*.

To actually use that information, we need structure. Not in a "color-coded planner or perish" kind of way but a flexible, personalized system you can actually stick with. Something that helps you focus, organize your work, and make better decisions about where your time, energy, and brainpower go.

There's a mental model I use for when I feel like I can't drop anything but also can't catch my breath—when I'm drowning in client projects and trying to write a book, run my business, plan my wedding, say yes to speaking gigs, and still have a life outside of my laptop (wild, I know). It helps me name what deserves my full attention, what can flow in the background, and what can be paused, delegated, or gracefully archived until later.

This system won't promise you balance. But it *will* help you prioritize with clarity, work in a way that actually makes sense for your brain, and help you feel less like you're drowning in a sea of Slack pings and half-finished Notion boards.

How It Works

Instead of labeling everything "urgent" or "high priority!!" and then wondering why you're so tired, behind, and low-key resenting your own ambition, split your workload into three fluid categories: (1) anchor projects, (2) current threads, and (3) slow burners.

Anchor Projects

These are your nonnegotiables. They are the high-impact, high-priority commitments that need your consistent time and energy. Maybe not forever but right now. They power your income, reputation, or creative momentum, and they get prime space on your calendar.

Think: paid client work, a product launch, an active consultancy, or a big speaking engagement you're prepping for.

Ask yourself: *If I dropped this tomorrow, what would fall apart?*

Current Threads

Still active, still important, but not demanding the majority of your time. These are the projects that hum along in the background. You touch them regularly but not obsessively. And maybe they have looser timelines or lower stakes.

Think: a podcast that runs seasonally, your newsletter, ops projects, community-building.

Ask yourself: *Am I actively doing this, or just "keeping it warm"?*

Slow Burners

The ideas that won't leave you alone ... but aren't also demanding any attention right now. These could be creative, strategic, or even personal in nature. You're not acting on them *yet*, but they're not off the table either. Slow burners live on the *back* burner until the timing aligns or you free up the bandwidth to do them justice.

Think: that nonprofit you want to start, the book you've been wanting to write for two years, that course or certification you want to take someday.

Ask yourself: *Do I feel guilty about this every time I open my laptop, like I could be working on something else instead?*

A Quick Look at My Structure (Right Now)

To bring this home, Table 9.3 shows a snapshot of how I've structured my own work using this method. (Remember: These categories shift! What's an anchor project today might be a current thread in three months.)

Some of these items move around depending on the season or week. LinkedIn content is occasionally an anchor; it helps build my credibility and audience. But now it's more of a current thread. Still valuable, still consistent, but not where most of my energy is going right now.

Table 9.3 Structure of My Work

Anchor Projects	Current Threads	Slow Burners
Client campaigns + consulting	My podcast(s)	Future events I've been dreaming up
Writing this book	LinkedIn content creation	A course I might build (eventually)
Influencer strategy + management	My newsletter (*This Could've Been an Email*)	Going back to school
Brand partnerships	Speaking gigs	Community concept

Start Building Yours

Now it's your turn. If you're unsure where to start, here's a step-by-step to help you.

Take Inventory

Brain dump everything you're doing or thinking about doing. Yes, everything. Don't censor yourself. Write out every project, commitment, and loose idea floating around in your head. From the clients you serve to the product you might launch one day to the idea you voice-noted yourself last month at 2:43 a.m.

Assign Each Item to a Category

Use the previous questions to guide you. Which items absolutely need your focus right now? Which ones are active but not top of mind? Which ones have been simmering quietly, waiting for their moment?

Anchor Projects	Current Threads	Slow Burners
Needs consistent attention and delivers high ROI (financial, strategic, emotional)	Matters to you, but doesn't need constant input (or output)	Future ideas or paused projects that you revisit occasionally
Client work, a major launch, a big consulting engagement	Newsletter, podcast, collaborations	Screenplay, new product/app idea, that course you want to build

Audit Your List

Be brutally honest with yourself:

- Are there too many things in your Anchor list? *Hello, burnout.*

- Are your Slow Burners actually things you don't want to do but feel guilty about? *Archive them. Permission granted.*

- Do your Current Threads reflect what you say your long-term goals are?

Look for Friction

Take note of the items that make your chest tighten or your energy dip. That's a clue. Either something needs to move categories or get dropped entirely. Don't keep things active out of obligation.

This framework gives you a living, breathing way to prioritize without guilt. You don't have to cut everything out all the time; you just have to give everything the placement and pacing they deserve. When things shift (and they will!), you update the table. Use this for clarity.

Mini Exercise: Shift One Thing

As I mentioned earlier, don't try to do a full overhaul of your life overnight. Just shift one thing.

- Move a current thread into *Slow Burner* status and give yourself the gift of not thinking about it for the next two months.

- Take something that's quietly become an Anchor and decide if it still deserves that title, or if it's just sitting there out of habit.

(continued)

(continued)

We don't need to be doing less just for the sake of it. We just need to know what we're doing and *why*. And when everything has its proper home, your brain can stop ping-ponging between "I should do more" and "I don't have time to do *anything*."

Letting Go Without Guilt

Once you've sorted through what's front and center and what can quietly sit in the background, a new kind of clarity starts to settle in. But clarity's annoying cousin sometimes comes along for the ride: guilt. Even after you've moved something to Slow Burner status or lovingly archived a dream that's not meant for this season, there's still that voice that pipes up.

You know the one. The one that says:

- *But you used to love this.*
- *But you already told people you were doing it.*
- *But what if you regret letting it go?*

But, but, but.

Let me be the one to say it: You don't owe your past self a life-long contract to any of your projects, dreams, or whims. Letting go doesn't mean you failed. It doesn't mean the idea wasn't good. It doesn't mean you didn't *really* want it at some point. It just means that you have new information now. You've grown. The context has shifted. Your priorities have evolved.

We love to romanticize "grit." Hustle culture has turned "toughing it out" into a virtue, like sticking with something long after it's served you is always the stronger choice. But sometimes, grit is just glorified burnout or pride in disguise.

One of the hardest things I've had to learn, over and over, is knowing when to quit. I've quit jobs that clashed with my values or didn't pay enough. I've walked away from passion projects that turned out to be dead ends. I exited a business partnership that wasn't the right fit. And each time, it felt complicated. But it was also the right call.

Quitting gets a bad rap. But sometimes, when we quit, we're not giving up. As one of my mentors once told me, "Sometimes when we quit, we're making room for something better." Better energy, better alignment, better opportunities.

Of course, not all quitting or "letting go" is brave. I've quit things out of fear too—fear of failing, fear of being seen, fear of proving myself right when I doubted that I could pull something off.

So now, before I walk away from anything, I ask myself two questions:

- Am I quitting because I'm afraid or because this no longer serves me?

- Is this decision coming from a scarcity mindset or from knowing what I need next?

Sometimes you don't need to push harder. You need to release your grip. You can thank a project for what it taught you and still walk away. You can put a dream on pause without lighting it on fire. And no, you don't have to explain your decisions to anyone who's not living your life, in your calendar, with your inbox, or paying your bills.

And *that* is how you protect your energy, your focus, and future.

Juggling multiple projects and careers can feel messy. It's not going to be perfect, and that's okay! The goal is to create a life that feels full, multifaceted, and uniquely yours. Plan your weeks. Block your time. Say no when you need to. Let go of the things that no longer serve you. You're curating a life that's as multifaceted and vibrant as you are.

Takeaways

- To make your career manageable, you need a structure that reflects how you actually work. Once you understand your rhythm, you can stop trying to "do it all" the hard way and start doing the right things in the right season.
- Labeling every project as urgent isn't a strategy. Knowing what deserves your full attention (and what doesn't) is how you will protect your energy and keep your work sustainable, fulfilling, and focused.
- Letting go is a leadership skill. When you curate your commitments instead of clinging to them out of guilt, fear, or ego, you create the space for deeper alignment, better results, and a career that grows with you.

Chapter 10

Unlocking the Invisible Income
You Didn't Know You Had

It's 8:30 p.m. on a Thursday. I'm sitting on my friend Naomi's couch, wine glass in hand, listening to her explain (again) why she doesn't have the time, resources, or energy to start a side hustle. "I mean, I don't have any useful skills anyway," she says, waving off my suggestion like the idea is a gnat buzzing too close to her face.

No skills?!

This is the same woman who planned an elaborate wedding on a budget, wrangled 20 of her close friends for a girls' trip to Mexico, and somehow convinced a luxury resort to upgrade our rooms just because she asked. The same woman who knows how to negotiate, budget, organize, and charm her way into any deal.

Invisible income, my friends. Invisible income.

We tend to assume that valuable skills must be formal—the things we learned in school, got certified for, or built entire careers around. But some of the most valuable, income-generating skills are things we do naturally, without even realizing their worth. Invisible income, put simply, defines all the expertise, resources, and opportunities sitting right under your nose. The things you do so naturally or have in such abundance that you don't even realize they have value.

Chances are, you already have something worth monetizing. You just might not see it yet. And now it's time to uncover what that is, dust it off, and see how it can quietly (yet powerfully) bolster your financial and career goals.

What Is Invisible Income?

Invisible income isn't a financial term you'll typically find in a textbook. It's not the check your great aunt forgot to put in your birthday card. It's definitely not a secret strategy for stocks. It's not even technically income yet—but it could be.

Invisible income is a term I'm using to describe something different. It's the value you've already created through your lived experiences, skills, instincts, and creativity that you haven't monetized yet. Mostly because you haven't yet realized its value.

It's the latent earning potential hiding in things that you do naturally. The stuff you've brushed off as "no big deal." The systems, resources, hacks, and superpowers you've built for yourself that would make someone else's life a whole lot easier ... if they knew about them. If you *let* them.

If it helps, think of it like this: You've already "earned" this potential through trial and error, job experiences, your side quests, and natural talent. You're just not cashing in on it yet.

Think of it like this:

- *Undervalued skills:* The problems you casually solve that others are stress-Googling at 2 a.m. The skills that are second nature to you. Just because they come naturally doesn't mean it's the same for everyone else.

- *Hobbies with hidden value:* Things you do for fun that others would pay for, learn from, or benefit from.

- *Personal systems and resources:* Spreadsheets, templates, work-flows, and/or strategies you've created that could benefit others and make their lives easier too.

So many of us walk around with entire toolkits in our heads and don't even realize it. We think, *That's just how I do XYZ.* Yeah. And that's why it matters. Because the way *you* do it is different. Easier. More efficient. More joyful. More intuitive. More effective. And someone else might need that exact resource, insight, or shortcut.

That's what this chapter is here for: to help you stop underestimating yourself and, instead, look at your own skill set, personal and professional, and ask, "Is there an opportunity here?"

Why We Overlook What Could Be Our Invisible Income

If you've never watched *Mad Men* … first of all, you're missing out. (I've probably watched the whole thing, all the way through, 20–25 times. What can I say, *it's a comfort show.*)

Peggy Olson, a main character, starts the show as Don Draper's secretary, with no real idea of her own potential. She's just doing what comes naturally: observing people, picking up on what they need and want, and occasionally suggesting ideas that make perfect sense to her.

In Season 1, she stumbles into writing copy for the Belle Jolie lipstick campaign. She casually describes the sample lipsticks as a "basket of kisses" and tosses out the phrase "Mark your man." To Peggy, it was instinct. To Don, it's talent worth nurturing. That moment sets her on the path to becoming one of the agency's best copywriters.

Most of us have had at least one moment in our lives where someone pointed out something we're naturally great at—something we do without thinking—and we just shrugged it off.

Maybe your friend gushed about how effortlessly you organize your travel itineraries, and you laughed it off with a casual, "Oh, I just like planning!" Or maybe a colleague came to you for advice on negotiating a raise, and after they walked away with a salary bump, you barely gave it a second thought.

We treat our strengths like background noise. As if, because we don't struggle with something, our expertise isn't worth anything. The most obvious opportunities don't look like opportunities. They look like habits or things you do on autopilot. Favors you casually do for friends that make their jaws drop and make you shrug like, "Wait, that's not normal?"

We normalize our own magic and devalue what comes naturally to us. But why?

You Might Be Too Good for Your Own Good

One of the weirdest, funniest things about being competent is that you tend to stop noticing it. Like, you've been organizing your Google Drive and color-coding your project management tools since 2017, and now you can't understand why your friend's desktop looks like a dumpster fire. Or you put together a strategy deck in 45 minutes and wonder why your manager is acting like you just discovered fire.

You know you're skilled. But your skills don't feel extraordinary to you anymore. They've become muscle memory. This is what I mean when I say we normalize our own magic. The things you're best at might not feel like work to you, so you assume they don't count, that they're not valuable, or—even worse—you think every-one else can do them too.

So, let's *un*-normalize your magic for a second and shine a light on it.

The "Too Good to Notice" Inventory

Open up your Notes app. Or grab your notebook if you're the pen-to-paper type. Let's start identifying the skills and assets that might quietly bankroll your next impactful opportunity.

Step 1: Do a self-audit. Break your thoughts into three categories:

People Always Ask Me For ...	I Built This Myself ...	I Do This Without Thinking ...
What do your friends, coworkers, and clients always come to you for? And be specific! If the group chat hits you up every time someone needs a résumé review, that counts.	What have you made that's helped you do something better, faster, easier, or smarter? Think about the systems, templates, and tools that you probably treat like "no big deal."	The intuitive stuff. What comes to you so naturally that you forget it's a skill? *Examples:* Explaining complex topics clearly. Naming things. Spotting design issues. Project management.

Unlocking the Invisible Income You Didn't Know You Had

If it helps, here is how this looks for me:

People Always Ask Me For ...	I Built This Myself ...	I Do This Without Thinking ...
• Polishing and rewriting LinkedIn profiles • Advice on writing and content creation • Naming projects, events, newsletters, etc. • Storytelling and brand strategy • Marketing strategy (and execution) • Event planning • Influencer marketing (strategy and execution) • Career advice for multi-hyphenates, entrepreneurs, and portfolio careerists	• DIY wedding planning spreadsheet (with full logistics, timelines, and run of show) • Creative briefs • Full marketing and content calendar templates • Multi-hyphenate career frameworks • Client onboarding processes • Talk outlines and keynote decks • Micro-event series concepts	• Capturing the exact right tone in writing • Naming and organizing frameworks/processes • Project management • Reading the emotional undercurrent of conversations or briefs • Coaching others through career pivots and mindset shifts • Turning a bunch of scattered ideas into a clear story

Step 2: Add color. Next to each item, add colors:

- *Green:* I enjoy this.
- *Purple:* I've made (or could make money) doing this.
- *Red:* I'd rather not do this ever again.

Don't overthink this part! Just follow the feeling.

Step 3: Spot the patterns. What overlaps do you see? Are there items you enjoy and could monetize? Are there things you're constantly asked for but never considered charging for?

Now look at the *Red* column. These are the things that might feel valuable but aren't aligned for you anymore. Great insight. Archive and move on.

So What Do You Do with This?

The purpose of this exercise is to get curious. What's already here that you're overlooking? If you spot something that's both *Green* and *Purple*, you might consider:

- Packaging it into a downloadable resource.
- Turning it into a service offering (even part-time).
- Teaching it via a workshop or webinar.
- Partnering with someone who needs what you can offer.

You don't have to scale everything or turn the entire list into a business. But the objective is to start noticing what's already working in your favor—and to stop defaulting to the belief that value only comes from struggle, sacrifice, or someone else's stamp of approval. When you stop underestimating your own instincts, systems, and weird little skill sets, you can start unlocking new paths. Ones that don't require starting from scratch, just looking at what you've already built and finally seeing it clearly.

We're Taught to Separate Work and Play

Somewhere between fourth grade and your first job, someone convinced you that work was supposed to feel like … well, work. Joy was extracurricular, and anything fun couldn't *possibly* count as serious or legitimate.

But some of the most successful ventures in the world have come from people tapping into what they enjoy. It doesn't have to be *all* about passion, but there's power in letting yourself break the mold of what "work" is supposed to look like.

Play and work aren't enemies. Think about the chef who finds joy in experimenting with flavors or a graphic designer who lights up when building a brand's visual identity. The magic happens when work and play get to sit at the same table, when we lean into the stuff that lights us up—and also recognize that it has actual, practical value. You don't need to love every minute of your work, but if you love parts of it—if you're energized by certain tasks, projects, or problems—that's worth exploring.

What Would You Do for Free?

Let's ditch the hypotheticals for a second. Sit back and imagine you had a few hours every week to help people with something. No compensation, no expectations, and no pressure to turn it into a business. What would you jump at?

Here are some ideas:

- Helping someone revamp their online presence.
- Helping a brand build pitch decks.
- Designing custom Notion databases.
- Organizing someone's closet or apartment.
- Planning the perfect vacation.

- Ghostwriting or editing someone's dating app messages (it's okay, we've all done it).

- Coordinating someone's cross-country move because you live for logistics.

- Helping a nonprofit clarify their messaging and storytelling.

Now flip the script: What are other people already doing for free, that they could be charging for? Look at your answers and ask: Who benefits from this? And what might it be worth to them?

To be clear, you're not committing to monetizing all of this. I'm just encouraging you to pay attention to what lights you up without being asked. That's where opportunity likes to hide.

We Don't Recognize the Market Signals

A lot of people aren't paying for a product or service just because they're paying for relief—convenience, confidence, shortcuts, time-savers. Anything that makes their lives easier or help them avoid pain, confusion, or overwhelm.

And you might already be building, doing, or sharing something people want. Remember, when I say, "invisible income," I'm not talking about mythical money that floats through the air. I'm talking about market demand that *you* haven't noticed yet.

You make your own pitch decks for freelance clients. A friend sees it and says, "Wait, do you have a template for this?" That's demand.

You planned a bachelor party, and strangers in a Facebook group started DMing you for your itinerary. *That's* demand.

Don't think you need a fleshed-out business plan or MBA to know when something is resonating with people. Comments, questions, DMs, friends saying, "You should really do this for real," are typically more than just compliments—they're soft pitches. Pay attention.

145

And when in doubt, remember: People pay for simplicity, speed, and convenience. If your skills can offer any of those, they're worth more than you think.

Your Invisible Income Doesn't Have to Be Invisible Anymore

My hope is that, by now, you're starting to see it: the skills you shrugged off, the systems you built without even realizing it, the instincts you thought were "no big deal."

All of that doesn't have to be invisible. And like I said, you don't have to turn every skill into a business. You don't have to monetize every hobby or turn every spreadsheet into a coaching program. (Please don't.) But you owe it to yourself to stop pretending that these skills are meaningless. You've spent years building a toolkit that's entirely your own—piece by piece, experience by experience, mistake by mistake, win by win. You didn't stumble into anything. You earned it.

And when you start recognizing it—when you really see it—you give yourself more choices, leverage, and freedom to build a career and life that actually fit the way you're wired.

So, the next time you catch yourself thinking or saying, "It's no big deal," pause. Ask yourself:

- What if this *is* a big deal, and I'm just too close to see it?
- What if the thing I take for granted is the exact thing someone else is struggling to figure out?
- What if there's an opportunity right in front of me, but I've been conditioned to overlook it because it feels "too easy"?

You don't have to find something new to chase, and you don't have to start from scratch. It's time to see what's already yours and remind yourself that you can do something powerful with it.

Takeaways

- What feels easy to you might be exactly what someone else is willing to pay for. And just because it comes easily, that doesn't mean it's not valuable. Your instincts, shortcuts, and skills aren't obvious to everyone, and that's what makes them powerful.
- Invisible income doesn't require you to chase something new. You just have to see what you already have *differently*. Sometimes the biggest opportunity is hidden inside the things you've always brushed off or overlooked.
- The skills, systems, and instincts you've built are assets, not accidents. You earned them; you didn't stumble into them. Give yourself more leverage, choices, and power over your own path.

Unlocking the Invisible Income You Didn't Know You Had

Chapter 11

Exploring the Line Between Passion and Profit

W e're living in the golden era of side hustles. Everyone's building something—an Etsy store, a Substack, brand partnerships, a coaching business. There's never been an easier time to monetize your skills, and with social media constantly showing us people turning their hobbies into six-figure businesses, it's easy to wonder: *Am I missing out?*

Over the years, I've heard something I'm sure you've heard as well: "If you're good at something, never do it for free."

It's always said with all the conviction of someone who's watched *The Dark Knight* a few too many times (no judgment because, same). And while I'll admit that it's a fun mantra (and an incredible movie), let me be the first to say … it's not *great* advice.

It starts innocently enough. You're doing something you love, and someone tells you, "You could *totally* make money doing this!" Suddenly, your peaceful knitting sessions turn into an Etsy store business plan. Your casual video editing hobby starts feeling like an untapped revenue stream. Before you know it, you're spiraling, wondering if you've been wasting your time not turning every skill into a business.

For years, I let that voice lead me astray. If I enjoyed something and someone suggested that I monetize it, I felt obligated to give it a shot. I mean, after all, isn't that the dream? To get paid for doing something you love (or at least like)? But here's the thing: not every passion needs to be a paycheck. Some things are better left as they are—joyful, personal, self-nourishing pursuits that are untouched by the stress of monetization.

The bigger question isn't "*Can* I monetize this?" It's "*Should* I monetize this?"

Let's talk about how to tell the difference.

The Pressure to Monetize: External Versus Internal Motivations

How do you know if you *actually want* to monetize something or if you just feel pressured to?

We live in a world where hobbies aren't really allowed to just be hobbies anymore. Everything has to be a *thing*. You can't just enjoy running—you have to train for a marathon. You can't just like baking—you have to start sharing your recipes on TikTok. You can't just paint for fun; you have to open an Etsy store, sell prints, and build a brand.

And suddenly, if you're doing something for fun, it feels … *wasteful?* Like you're leaving money on the table, and that's just unacceptable.

Keep in mind that there's a difference between intrinsic motivation (*I genuinely want to explore this as a business*) and external pressure (*Everyone's saying I should, so … maybe I should?*). One is a fire that comes from within. The other is like being gently shoved onto a stage you never signed up to perform on. Yikes.

Let's break it down.

External Pressure: Monetization as an Expectation

With external pressure, someone tells you, "You should totally sell this!" But instead of feeling inspired, you feel weirdly guilty for not monetizing. You see other people monetizing something similar, and now you're wondering if you're "behind."

Monetization feels more like a responsibility than an opportunity.

If you didn't post about it, would you still feel as excited about doing it?

Internal Motivation: Monetization as a Natural Progression

With internal motivation, you feel genuinely pulled toward the idea of monetizing something. It excites you—not just the idea of money but the process itself.

You would still do it, even if no one was watching or validating it. The thought of growing it into something bigger is potentially energizing, not exhausting.

If you were the only person in the world who knew about your skills, you'd still feel drawn to build something.

See the difference? External pressure makes you feel like monetization is an obligation. Internal motivation makes it feel like an opportunity. External factors can open your eyes to a new opportunity, but the final decision should come from excitement, not guilt.

How to Determine If Monetization Is Worth It

Before you start turning your project into a paycheck, it's worth taking a step back and asking yourself some key questions:

- *Would I still enjoy this if I had to do it on a schedule?*
  Hobbies are fun partly because they're optional. If this became a daily or weekly responsibility, do you think you'd struggle to find motivation? Or would it still interest you?

- *Am I willing to handle the behind-the-scenes work?*
  Unless you have a strong support system that has offered to take on some of the duties and responsibilities, every side hustle and/or business has tasks that are less fun. If you don't want to deal with those, running a business around this skill might not be for you.

- *Do I need this to be my main source of income?*
  If yes, you need a plan. A real one. Because "fun" alone won't pay the bills. If not, you have the luxury of keeping it low-pressure or experimental.

- *Will turning this into a side hustle change how I feel about this?*
  Be honest with yourself. Some things are worth protecting and are meant to be just for you.

At the end of the day, there are a million ways that you can monetize and diversify your income. So sometimes, it's not about whether you *can* make money doing something. It's about whether you actually *want to.*

So how do you separate the "This could be a great revenue stream" from the "This should stay a hobby"? This is where the three-minute test comes in. It helps you evaluate your ideas and pursuits and helps you decide if you want to monetize them.

But before I walk you through that exercise, let me tell you a story.

My T-shirt and Bucket Hat Debacle

A few years ago, I entered a graphic t-shirt and bucket hat phase. You know the ones—bold slogans, fun designs, the kind that make people do a double take.

So, I started creating my own just for fun. A cheeky slogan here, a fun design there. It was low-stakes, creative, and a cool way to change up my wardrobe without struggling to find what I wanted online. I'd design them in Canva, order a few through a print-on-demand site, and wear them whenever I felt like it.

Then the comments started rolling in: "Oh my god, where did you get that?" "You should totally sell these!" "Can I buy one?"

At first, I laughed it off. But after hearing it over and over again, I started to wonder, "Could this be a business?"

So, I gave it a shot. I set up an online store, uploaded a few of my designs, and started dreaming of stardom and fame. And let me tell you, the reality of selling t-shirts was not nearly as fun as making them. Suddenly, I wasn't just creating for me anymore. I was:

- tracking orders and answering customer questions;
- planning out photo shoots, booking models, and negotiating with influencers;
- spending hours figuring out profit margins and new designs; and
- answering endless customer emails: *Can I request something custom? When will my order ship? Do you offer discounts for bulk orders?*

What was once my happy little creative outlet had turned into a source of anxiety. And honestly, I already had enough of those. When I sat back and thought about it, I just wasn't enjoying myself, and I wasn't committed to the process. So, I shut it down. I went back to making t-shirts and hats for myself. And it became fun again.

Just because people tell you to monetize something doesn't mean it's the right move. Some things are worth keeping sacred because they bring you happiness, not profit. And if you do want to monetize something you're working on, do the work first to determine if it's the right decision.

Exploring the Line Between Passion and Profit

The Three-minute Test

My t-shirt business taught me something: When you're deciding whether to monetize a skill/passion/project or not, you need to do a gut check. Fast, simple, and brutally honest.

I call that gut check the *Three-minute Test*. Pick the thing that you're thinking about monetizing; then, set a timer for three minutes. Now answer three questions:

1. Would I still love doing this if I had to do it on someone else's timeline?

2. If I made zero dollars in the first six months, would I still be proud of what I built?

3. Am I more excited about the thing itself or the idea of being "seen" doing the thing?

The last one is brutal (and maybe a little painful), but it's so necessary. Better that it's painful now, instead of two years into building a brand you secretly can't stand. If you're hemming and hawing, writing long-winded "pros and cons" lists, or already finding ways to explain it away, you've got your answer. But remember what I always say: It doesn't have to be a no forever. But it's probably a "no" for now.

If your answers roll out fast, clear, and excited, without feeling the need to justify it to yourself, congratulations. You've probably found something worth pursuing.

If I had given myself a three-minute gut check back then, I might've saved myself from a lot of stress (and a whole lot of shipping drama—don't ask). So, let's rewind for a second and break down exactly where my business would have landed.

Back to My T-shirt and Bucket Hat Business

Designing my t-shirts and bucket hats was fun. Selling them was a nightmare. If I had run my business idea through the Three-minute Test back then, it would've been obvious.

- *Would I still love doing this if I had to do it on someone else's timeline?* Nope. The moment orders started rolling in, the fun drained out. Deadlines, customer emails, shipping mishaps. It stopped being creative and started feeling like a second job I didn't remember applying for. Surprise, surprise.

- *If I made zero dollars in the first six months, would I still be proud of what I built?* Absolutely not. I wasn't trying to design a brand that I deeply believed in. I was making fun t-shirts because it made *me* happy. So, when I started putting pressure on myself to sell more, more, more, I didn't have anything to cling to. Slapping a checkout button on my designs didn't magically turn it into a mission I cared about—unless the mission was to develop a deep resentment toward Shopify notifications.

- *Am I more excited about the thing itself or the idea of being "seen" doing the thing?* I would not have been able to answer this question because I wasn't actually sure why I was running my passion project as a business in the first place.

My final verdict: Even if I made a few bucks here and there, the actual cost—in energy, time, and existential dread—wasn't worth it. Unless the payoff included free therapy and a personality transplant, it was never going to make sense. So, once I shut it down and went back to making t-shirts for myself, it was fun again. I ditched the metrics and forgot about profit margins. Just me, Canva, and an unreasonable amount of custom bucket hats. Perfect.

The Case for "Boring" Side Hustles

Maybe you've realized that your dream gig isn't quite realistic yet or that some of your most profitable skills don't exactly feel sustainable for you. Now what?

Let me introduce to you one of the most underrated (and highly effective) strategies out there: *boring side hustles.*

Let's be real. Not every side hustle will feel super cool or Instagram-worthy. They're not designed to land you on a "30 Under 30" list, go viral, or land you a *Forbes* feature. Some are simple, unassuming, and sometimes even a little dull.

But boring makes money.

Some of the most successful, profitable, and sustainable side hustles aren't flashy. They won't necessarily make for exciting small talk at a party, but they *will* pay your bills, fund your other projects, and give you financial stability to take bigger swings elsewhere.

And if you need proof that "boring" can be lucrative, look no further than some of the most tried-and-true income streams:

- *Dog-sitting and dog walking:* Reliable, in demand, and recession-proof. People will *always* need someone to take care of their pets. My good friend Kristin and her husband have been dog-sitting through Rover for years, and they make a pretty penny doing it.

- *Vending machines:* A classic passive income play.

- *Tutoring:* If you're great at math, writing, test prep, etc., people will pay a premium to have you help their kids.

Tori Dunlap, personal finance expert and founder of Her First $100K, started her first business as a side hustle with a gumball vending machine. When she was nine years old, her dad bought it for her. And as she reinvested her earnings into more vending machines, she learned how to manage inventory, maximize profits, and grow a business. Today, she runs a multimillion-dollar personal finance company.

The lesson here: "Boring" might just be the smartest move you'll ever make.

Find Your Boring Side Hustle

You don't need a million-dollar idea. Sometimes, you just need a low-risk, steady way to bring in extra income. One that frees up your time, reduces financial stress, and funds the things you *actually* care about.

So, let's brainstorm some potential side hustles. Look for things that check off these boxes:

- *Low startup costs* (No major investments needed to get going.)
- *Consistency* (Does this meet an ongoing need for someone?)
- *Flexibility* (Can you fit this into your current schedule?)
- *Scalability* (Could this grow if you wanted it to? This one is not mandatory—not every gig or project has to grow into a huge conglomerate.)

Now, pick one or two that feel doable and experiment.

Not every side hustle will be a perfect fit, and that's okay. The goal is to start small, test the waters, and see what actually works. You do not need to find your "forever business."

And once you start seeing income trickle in from something low-lift or "boring," it opens up a much bigger question: What else could you be monetizing if you actually wanted to?

Why Monetize?

Look, you don't *have* to monetize anything. No one's going to show up at your door with a clipboard and a *You Failed Capitalism* stamp if you keep your watercolor hobby or Excel wizardry to yourself.

But sometimes, making money off something you're already good at just feels … good. And if your concern is that you're "selling out," let me stop you right there. You're not. You're buying yourself some breathing room. And honestly, a little breathing room can change everything.

When you choose to monetize a skill on your own terms, it can crack open a whole new set of possibilities. And not just the "quit your job and live on a beach in Bali" variety that Instagram keeps trying to sell you. It's bigger (and better) than that. Let's talk about it.

The Upsides of Monetizing (Besides, You Know, Money)

There are many upsides to monetizing:

- *It gives you options.* First of all, you'll never catch me saying, "Well, money doesn't buy happiness." Most people who say that are … pretty wealthy. In my opinion, money doesn't fix all of your problems, but it can make them less claustrophobic. (And as my friend Keli used to say, "I'd rather cry in a Porsche.")

  When you build even a *small* income stream on your own terms, you're stacking cash, but you're also stacking *options* for yourself:

  - Options to quit faster.
  - Options to pivot smarter.
  - Options to say, "Actually, no thank you," without spiraling into financial ruin.

    Freedom doesn't always come from a lottery ticket. Sometimes it comes from quietly stacking $300 a month on the side until you can make a bigger move.

- *It turns your strengths into assets.* You've already built, or are building, the instincts and skills. You don't have to keep handing them out like free samples at Costco just because. Treat your talents like they have weight—because they do.

- *It builds proof (and momentum).* Your first $50 sale is about more than the $50. It's when you realize, "Oh. I actually know what I'm doing."

It's proof, tangible evidence, that you know what you're doing. And that you're building something that someone else sees value in, even if it's small, even if it's messy, and even if you're still secretly Googling things like "How to send a QuickBooks invoice" at 1 a.m.

After that, and over time, it gets easier to bet on yourself and harder to listen to the voice in your head that says you're making it all up as you go (even if you are). The truth is, a lot of people are making it up as they go. The difference is that you have receipts now.

Sometimes, that's all you need to stop second-guessing yourself and start stacking tiny wins into real momentum.

When It Might Make Sense to Monetize

Sometimes, the decision to monetize is less about the money and more about momentum. You've been noodling on an idea for months. You've built something useful or interesting. People are asking for it. And *deep down*, you're ready to see what it can become.

In my experience, that's usually your cue.

Monetization can be a way to test the waters without jumping into the deep end. It's how you learn what people actually want, what you enjoy delivering, and whether the gap between those two things is a bridge or a brick wall. You don't need a master plan—just a willingness to take it seriously enough to try.

Exploring the Line Between Passion and Profit

It also makes sense when the following are true:

- You're already doing the work for free, and people keep asking for more.

- You want more autonomy or financial breathing room.

- You're looking for a stepping stone to leave a role, shift careers, or fund something bigger.

- You're itching to create something that's truly yours and see where it leads.

This is about traction. Building momentum. Earning your first dollar online—or your first $500—to prove to yourself that the idea has legs and that you know how to move forward.

That small shift in energy is a powerful one.

A Quick Reality Check

That first sale might not be life changing. But it *is* self-changing. That first Stripe notification hits different. It's confirmation that your idea can hold weight outside your own head, that your instincts might be right, and that you're capable of building something people actually want.

Choosing to monetize something is about recognizing that your skills, systems, little talents, and creative brain already have value—and sometimes, letting them pay you back a little for everything they've already helped you build.

But—and it's a big but—monetization comes with fine print that people don't post about on LinkedIn and Instagram. So, before you set up your Stripe account and announce your new side hustle, we should talk about what's *actually* happening behind those "six-figure side hustle" headlines.

Let's get into the part that nobody warns you about, so you can make the best decision for *you*.

The Hidden Costs of Monetization

So, let's say you take the plunge and decide to turn something into a revenue stream. What's the worst that could happen?

A lot, actually.

We tend to romanticize the upside of monetization. Extra income, a potential career shift, financial freedom. But what about the trade-offs? What happens if something that once felt liberating starts feeling like another obligation?

Turning something you're passionate about (or even just interested in) into a revenue generator is about more than just adding an extra income. It can change the entire relationship you have with that thing or project. Suddenly, it's not just about the creative process. It's about what sells, what scales, what meets demand. You're no longer just doing the *fun part*. You're also potentially handling logistics, customer service, marketing, pricing, and the admin work that comes with running a side hustle or business.

I'm not trying to scare you off, but I do want to make sure you're considering all angles. Starting a side hustle can be an incredible move, but it does come with trade-offs. Knowing them upfront can help you decide if it's worth it for you.

When a hobby becomes a business, the experience shifts. What was once a personal creative escape now comes with expectations: deadlines, customers, and the pressure to keep up. And sometimes, that can change how it feels. Here's what can happen:

- *You're not just doing the fun part anymore.* Like we talked about before—the moment you start selling something, you're not just focused on creation or production anymore. You're managing everything around it. Marketing, emails, inventory, bookkeeping, customer services, taxes. The work behind the work can become just as consuming as the thing itself.

161

- *Monetization can kill the enjoyment.* When you *have* to do something, it can sometimes change your relationship with it. A project that once felt energizing can start to feel like a chore.

- *Income can be inconsistent.* Some months, sales might be booming. Others? Silence. Unless you have a strong foundation, your income can be unpredictable, which means stress, financial pressure, and a different kind of hustle.

- *Just because you love your new side hustle doesn't mean it'll sell.* Talent and passion don't guarantee profit. The market has to exist. You have to price it right. And even then, success isn't immediate or guaranteed. Plenty of people create incredible work that never finds customers—not because they're not talented but because the demand isn't there. And unless you're strategic about pricing, expenses, and demand, you could end up putting in way more effort than the income is worth.

The lesson here is that monetization is a commitment. Yes, you can do what you love, but are you willing to take on everything that comes with it?

You don't owe every skill or spark of inspiration a business plan. But if there's something that's pulling at you—something you enjoy, people ask for, and/or you could see yourself building into something meaningful—then try it.

And remember, not everything needs to be forever. But everything you try gives you information, and clarity is its own kind of currency.

Takeaways

- Monetization is a tool, not a destination. You don't have to chase a full-blown business or scale to a conglomerate to give your skills value. Charging for your work can simply be a way to test ideas, expand your options, or build leverage on your own terms.

- Small income streams can open big doors. It doesn't have to be the next billion-dollar idea either. A few hundred dollars a month from something can fund your exit plan, build your confidence, or make your day-to-day feel less financially tight.
- When in doubt, try the Three-minute Test. Ask yourself: Would I still want to do this if it came with deadlines? Would I still be proud if I didn't earn a dime? Am I in love with the thing or just the idea of being seen doing the thing? Your gut already knows. Your job is to listen.

Exploring the Line Between Passion and Profit

Chapter 12

Navigating What to Do When You Feel Like You've Lost Your "Why"

When I first launched my business Verbatim, it was shiny and new, full of potential, and terrifyingly real.

I didn't start it alone—I actually had a business partner. Together, we mapped out the vision, landed our first clients, and hit the ground running. It was exhilarating. It was intense. It felt like *this* was the thing we were meant to build.

Then, around month three, the cracks started to show. Our priorities didn't match. Our work styles didn't complement each other. Our goals weren't aligning. Even our *whys*—the reasons we started the business in the first place—didn't actually match up. And once you start noticing those misalignments, you can't *un*see them. At first, I brushed it off as growing pains. But by month six, the business partnership ended.

To a great extent, breaking up with a business partner feels like breaking up with a romantic partner—but instead of deciding who gets to keep the air fryer, you're untangling financials, business assets, and the thing you've spent months (or years) building together. Every detail had to be dealt with, and every decision felt heavy. It was frustrating. It was draining. It was sad. Once the dust settled, I found myself sitting at my desk, staring at the screen, wondering if I'd made the right decision. Could I actually do this on my own? Or should I just cut my losses?

Then my fiancé (now husband) hit me with *the* most annoying, yet necessary, question: "Why did you start this business in the first place?"

Cue the eye roll. *Sir, can I have my dramatic spiral in peace?* But he had a point. I wanted to build something meaningful, something that was *mine*. I wanted to help brands grow in a way that felt human, that celebrated inclusivity and good marketing. And I wanted to create good, human content that mattered.

That hadn't changed. The circumstances had. The partnership had. My energy had. But the core reason I'd launched Verbatim was still there. I'd just let the situation cloud my vision. Once I remembered that, everything felt clearer.

That's the thing about losing your "why." Rarely does it mean that you chose wrong. More often than not, it means it's time to reset, realign, and remember what you were building in the first place. So, if this is where you're at right now, just know that it isn't the end of the world. You're just at a crossroads.

Welcome to the "What am I even doing with my life?" stage. It's not fun, but you're not alone. And it's also not the end.

When Purpose Starts to Shift

There's a common myth that once you've found your "why," it stays locked in—unshakable, unchanging, immune to doubt. Cute idea. Totally unrealistic.

This idea of "purpose" can shift. It stretches with you, shifts with your priorities, and sometimes slips out of view when you're knee-deep in the chaos of work or life. And it gets reshaped by what you've lived through, what you've let go of, and what you're starting to want more of.

Losing your "why" can feel disorienting, but it's more common than we admit. People don't always talk about it, but it happens. Even the most passionate, driven, purpose-fueled people hit walls. The spark fades, the clarity slips, the work that used to feel energizing starts to feel distant, and motivation becomes harder to grab onto.

But, good news! That doesn't mean you've messed up. It doesn't mean you picked the wrong path. It just means something underneath the surface is trying to get your attention. Sometimes it means you need a new challenge. Sometimes you've outgrown an old definition of success or purpose. And *sometimes*, you just need to get reacquainted with what made you care in the first place. The key is figuring out what your instincts are trying to tell you before you confuse discomfort with failure or evolution with indecision.

This is the moment to get honest with yourself—with a grounded check-in, not another to-do list. What's feeling off? What used to light you up that now feels dim? Where's the friction showing up, and what can we learn from it?

Let's find out.

Understand What You're *Actually Feeling*

Are you burnt out? Have you outgrown the work? Or is it something else entirely?

When work stops feeling "right," most people try to throw solutions at it without figuring out what the actual problem is. They book a weekend getaway, buy a new planner, download that new mindfulness app, start a whole newsletter about burnout recovery (just me?). But clarity doesn't always come from productivity hacks. It comes from being honest, *especially* when the answer isn't clean or easy.

Burnout is one possibility. But not the only one. You could be burnt out. You could've outgrown what you're doing. You might be bored. You might have let someone else's definition of success hijack your own. Or maybe the version of yourself who built this brand/career/business isn't the version of you who wants to maintain it. All of those are valid, and they each come with different implications.

The tricky part is that burnout and detachment often show up wearing the same outfit. They both show up as apathy, distraction, and that familiar "ugh" that hits every time you open your laptop. But burnout says, "I want to care. I just physically and emotionally can't." It's a deletion problem, and it requires actual rest. I'm talking real, systems-level changes to how you're working.

Outgrowing your work sounds more like, "Even when I'm rested, this still doesn't feel like mine anymore." You're not drained per se—you're disconnected. You've evolved, but your work hasn't caught up yet. No spa day or sabbatical is going to solve that (believe me, I've tried that).

And then there's another category that doesn't get nearly enough airtime: disillusionment. You might still love the *idea* of what you do, but the day-to-day reality has shifted so far from the original spark that you struggle to recognize it. This category sneaks up on high achievers in particular. Everything looks great on paper … so why are you fantasizing about moving to a cabin in the woods and never opening Slack again?

The goal here is *not* to sit down and diagnose yourself like a Buzzfeed quiz (although I love those). The goal is to name what you're actually feeling so that you can respond accordingly. Each version of misalignment asks for something different: rest, reinvention, recommitment, or release. So, let's ask the harder questions and trace the discontent to its source. Clarity isn't always comfortable, but it *is* how you move forward.

Conduct an Honesty Audit

Take stock of where you are. Do a brain dump of everything you feel about your work right now. It doesn't have to be tidy. Just do a full download of how you *actually* feel about your work right now. The parts that thrill you, the parts that drain you, the stuff you brag about, and the stuff you quietly dread.

Once you conduct your audit, commit it to paper or a Notes app and scan through it, almost like you're editing a stranger's work. Here's what to flag:

- The stuff that makes you feel awake, present, or maybe even excited
- The pieces that feel flat, obligatory, or safe but stale
- The recurring patterns: projects or dynamics you've tried to "fix" more than twice

To help you with this audit, here's an illustration of what the finished product could look like:

Name: Jordan

Role: Full-time brand strategist and freelance designer

What I'm Feeling Right Now

- Dread when I open my inbox
- Annoyed by client revisions that don't feel like collaborations anymore
- Excited by the idea of working on my own project (maybe a template shop?)
- Jealous of peers launching courses and digital products
- Tired but sleeping fine, so it's not exhaustion

(continued)

Navigating What to Do When You Feel Like You've Lost Your "Why"

(continued)

What Still Feels Energizing

- Leading brand strategy for small, values-driven businesses
- Teaching design students and mentoring new grads
- Making content for Instagram

What Feels Like a Burden

- Back-to-back client calls
- Brand strategy retainers that drag on forever
- Endless rounds of feedback with clients that just don't "get it"
- Marketing myself—it feels performative lately

What I Quietly Dread

- Slack messages at 8 p.m.
- Running someone else's brand playbook
- Being "on" all the time for my clients and my team

Jordan's audit tells us that they crave more creative autonomy and less client handholding. Maybe they're not done with design, but they're tired of the agency model. And it sounds like they want to shift toward teaching and product creation but need to wean off client work gradually.

This exercise might sound overly simplistic, but clarity starts with honesty. If the goal is to help you *name the friction* that you're feeling, then you need to have a brutally clear snapshot of where you are right now—emotionally, mentally, and energetically—when it comes to your work.

Every job, business, or creative pursuit has friction. But the friction that repeats itself is usually trying to teach you something.

Rewind the Tape

Now that you've dumped the current stage of things onto a page and flagged what feels off, let's rewind a bit.

Look back at when things felt aligned—when you were energized, proud, or actually excited to talk about your work without immediately adding, "but it's been a rough couple of months." What were you building toward? What version of success had your attention back then? Zoom in on that stretch of time.

Maybe you were chasing a clear mission. Maybe you were just lit up by the learning curve. Maybe the pace worked. Maybe it was the people. Now stack that against where you are now. See any gaps or overlap?

Redefine Success (on Your Own Terms)

Some of us lose our sense of purpose, or our "why," not because it's gone, but because we've let external expectations hijack it. A while back, I chatted with a creator who had started a social media agency. She was making good money, landing great clients, and hitting all her goals. But about halfway through our conversation, she sighed and said, "It just doesn't feel the way I thought it would."

"What doesn't feel right?" I asked. And as she started to unpack her feelings, the answer became clear.

The version of success she was chasing wasn't even hers. She started her agency to help small businesses, primarily women owned. But after months of seeing agency owners celebrate their $100K months on LinkedIn, she started chasing bigger clients, bigger contracts, and a version of success she didn't *actually* want.

It's easy to get caught up in someone else's dream—to measure ourselves against someone else's highlight reel. But when was the last time you defined success for yourself and recalibrated accordingly?

Try This: Define Your *Right Now* Success

1. List three moments when you've felt most fulfilled in your work. What were you doing? Who were you helping? What felt good about it?

2. Describe what success looks like for you today. Not five years ago. Not last year. Right now. What do you actually want in this season of your life? (And if you don't know, that's okay too! Just write what feels *possible* for now.)

3. If no one else knew what you were doing, would you still want to do it? This one might sting a little, but it's worth exploring. Strip away the external validation, the LinkedIn announcements, the "look at me" moments. Would you still be on this path?

Redefining success for yourself is one of the fastest ways to reconnect with your sense of purpose. Because when your goals actually align with what *you* want, it's a lot harder to lose sight of them.

Knowing When to Pivot

Losing your "why" doesn't have to be a crisis. Sometimes it's actually an invitation to evolve.

But here's the catch: As a society, we tend to be a little extreme when it comes to change. On the one hand, we treat it like failure. If something isn't working, we guilt ourselves into pushing through, clinging to what once made sense. On the other hand, society *loves* to encourage a dramatic exit. Hate your job? Quit! Bored with your business? Burn it to the ground!

The truth is, most of us don't have the luxury of making instant, sweeping changes. As unsexy as it sounds, we have bills.

Responsibilities. People counting on us. In my case, I also have two spoiled dogs that have become accustomed to a certain type of lifestyle. And sometimes, we just need to ride out a rough patch. But that doesn't mean we have to stay stuck forever.

So, let's ditch the all-or-nothing thinking and talk about how to pivot with intention.

Know the Difference Between a "Funk" and a Real Need for Change

Just because something doesn't excite you *right now* doesn't mean you have to be done with it forever. Work, even when you love it, isn't always fun. Every business, job, or creative pursuit has its seasons. Some are exciting, some are slow, and some are downright exhausting.

So, before you declare a dramatic exit, let's take a step back and assess:

- Is this a passing phase, or has this been an ongoing struggle?

- Am I reacting to short-term frustration, or is this a long-term misalignment?

If you're in a rough season, the answer might be adjusting your workflow, setting stronger boundaries, or shifting priorities, not walking away entirely. But if you've been feeling this way for months (or even years), and if the idea of doing this forever makes you want to fling your laptop out the window, it might be time to start planning your exit strategy.

Recognize the Need for an Exit Strategy

A few summers ago, I hired a career coach. At the time, I was working in-house, and I wasn't trying to quit my job. I was trying to survive it.

I convinced myself that if I could just learn to manage up, find little moments of joy, become a stronger leader, fix my attitude, I'd feel better. But in our very first session, my new coach said the quiet part out loud: "It sounds like you don't want to fix your job. It sounds like you want to leave it and work for yourself."

She wasn't wrong. I didn't feel burnt out—I just felt done. Corporate wasn't a match anymore, and deep down, I knew that. But I also had bills and responsibilities. I couldn't just send a "Thanks for everything, but I'm out!" email and hope for the best. So instead of rage-quitting, I built a plan.

For the next three to four months, I quietly mapped out my exit strategy:

- I reworked my finances and cut unnecessary expenses.

- I started laying the foundation for my new business.

- I clarified what I actually wanted from work—creatively, logistically, and emotionally.

- I built a runway long enough to keep me calm when things got chaotic.

And just as I was gearing up to put in my notice—bam—I got laid off. But instead of spiraling, I hit "send" on my LLC paperwork.

That moment taught me something important: You don't have to fall in love with your job to stay in it for a while. But if you've named the friction and know you want to move on, start planning out your next steps.

How to Build a Smart Exit Strategy (Without Burning Everything Down)

The following strategies can be used to build a smart exit strategy:

- *Map out your timeline.* Are you trying to be out in three months? A year? Sooner? Great. Work backward. That gives you a planning window for income, savings, testing ideas, or updating your résumé without panic-quitting.

- *Let your next move fund itself.* Rather than quitting cold turkey, start testing the waters. Pick up a freelance project, start networking in a new industry, or build a side hustle that *eventually* lets you walk away, if that's your long-term goal. It's okay to start small. Treat this season like R&D.

- *Find someone who can identify and challenge your blind spots.* A coach, mentor, or even a brutally honest friend can help you see the stuff that's too close for you to name. You don't need to join a $10K mastermind (unless you want to). But you do need someone with a growth mindset, perspective, and the ability to clinically analyze your situation.

Staying in a role, or with a project, while you plan your pivot means that you're moving deliberately, not that you're settling. It's important to give yourself space to experiment, explore, and walk toward something with your eyes open—without torching your timeline or finances in the process. Make peace with the fact that your next chapter might be a slow build.

Purpose Isn't a Solo Project

When I was building Verbatim in the aftermath of the partnership ending, I had a lot of "Am I doing this right?" moments. Most of which happened late at night, while staring at a half-written client proposal and questionable bank balance.

One of the smartest things I did during that season was put the spiral on pause until I could phone a friend or mentor the next day. I reached out to a few people who knew me well enough to call me on my self-doubt but also had enough distance to see things I couldn't. One of those conversations helped me realize that I was scared, not confused or lost. Another reminded me of something I'd said in passing, months earlier, that actually held the key to my next move. And each conversation sharpened my own clarity.

Getting realigned can be powerful, but it's easy to stall when you're trying to realign in isolation. Without sounding boards, everything starts to feel louder and more tangled than it really is. Self-reflection turns into spiraling. Plans start to stretch into hypotheticals. And doubt turns into, "What am I even doing with my life?"

Not everything can, or should, be fixed in community, but it helps to check your blind spots with people who are rooting for your growth, not just your comfort. Ground yourself in a circle that reflects your values back to you, *especially* when your internal compass is foggy.

Whether you're at the beginning of a potential pivot or deep in the middle of it, here are some steps you can take to help build that support system:

- *Choose people who ask better questions.* Not just "What do you want to do?" but "What's actually working for you right now?" "What feels forced?" "What are you done pretending to care about?" The right mentors and community won't necessarily rush to fix you. They'll slow you down long enough to see clearly.

- *Rotate the mirror.* Share your Honesty Audit, your voice notes, your messy thoughts. Get feedback from someone who doesn't have a stake in your decision but *does* understand the weight of it.

- *Be explicit about what kind of support you need.* Sometimes it's a gut check. Sometimes it's tactical help. Sometimes it's just, "Tell me I'm not losing it." People can't show up if they don't know what showing up looks like.

- *Revisit your community map.* Do you have people for different seasons, someone to call when you want to burn it all down? Is there someone who'll remind you why you built it in the first place? This is about building a network and, more important, an ecosystem. Don't treat this season of your life like a secret you have to decode all alone. Share the puzzle. Let people help you rearrange the pieces.

Purpose evolves. It stretches, rewrites itself, and asks you to do the same. When your vision feels distant or your momentum stalls, sometimes it means you're due for a reset. Sometimes it means it's time to move on. But when things stop clicking, don't panic. Treat it as a sign that you need awareness, realignment, and a little bit of nerve.

If this chapter gave you clarity, good. If it poked at something you've been avoiding, even better. You've got momentum. Don't waste it.

Takeaways

- Losing your "why" is often a signal for growth or realignment. You haven't lost the plot, but maybe your pace needs adjusting, or your priorities have shifted. That's information you can work with.
- Reconnecting with your "why" starts by questioning old definitions of success. The clearer you are on what you actually want now—not what you said you wanted five years ago—the easier it becomes to find your way forward.
- Realignment is a team sport. Don't feel like you have to untangle all of this alone. Surround yourself with people who challenge your blind spots, help you protect your energy, and hold space while you recalibrate.

Chapter 13

Owning Your Version of Professionalism

It's a Friday evening, and I'm meeting a colleague and friend for an early dinner. In front of me, talking to the hostess, is a man in a tailored suit. His shoes are shined, his tie is knotted, and his watch looks like it costs more than my first car (or my second). For a split second, I wonder if he's what people imagine when they think of *professional*.

Then I catch a glimpse of my reflection in the restaurant window. Long Havana twists, tattoos on full display with my white tee, and nails that look more like mini works of art than anything you'd find in a corporate handbook.

And you know what? I'm just as professional as he is.

Seriously, What Does *Professionalism* Even Mean?

When was the first time you were told to "be professional"? What did it mean? Were you expected to lower your voice? Dress a certain way? And most important, how did that expectation make you feel?

For most of us, myself included, this idea of "professionalism" has always felt like something handed down from above. Rigid, impersonal, and full of unwritten expectations about how you should dress, how you should speak, how often you should job-hop, whether you're deemed to be "serious" enough about your career … the list goes on and on. But, if you ask me, these rules and expectations seem designed to exclude rather than include. If we think about it, the "ideal professional" was usually synonymous with being male, White, able-bodied, and cisgender. Anyone outside that mold was expected to contort themselves to fit.

But who benefits from these outdated definitions?

While professionalism used to mean fitting into someone else's mold, it doesn't have to be that way anymore. Professionalism can, and should, be something we define for ourselves, rooted in integrity, respect, and delivering value while showing up authentically. Our quest to redefine this is about liberation. It's about what you bring to the table and how you navigate your work, not what you wear or how linear your career path is. But how do we get there? And how do we navigate a world where these outdated norms still hold real power?

Think about it. Professionalism shifts depending on the room you're in. Corporate board room. Tech startup. Production set. Classroom. Zoom. Even regionally, the signals change. Each room carries its own set of expectations—sometimes written, sometimes implied, almost always contradictory. Professionalism has never been a fixed standard. It's a moving target. And the more we try to hit every version, the easier it is to lose our own definition. The more ambiguous the rules, the more pressure there is to conform. To decode and perform. To keep your edges polished and your individuality tucked away, just in case someone sees it as "too much."

We need to unpack your ideas about professionalism and determine whether those ideas still serve you. Because if you're holding yourself to an outdated or inherited standard, you're not building a career. You're performing.

The Cost of Chasing the Mold

So now we've talked about how the definition of professionalism shape-shifts across industries, cultures, and expectations. But for many of us, especially those who don't fit the default mold, these shifting definitions are more than just confusing. They're costly. Conforming comes at a price, and that price is often authenticity. I learned this the hard way.

When I was 25, I applied for a position at a company I was genuinely excited about. On the call with the recruiter, her voice practically sang through the phone. She raved about my résumé, said they were excited and eager to move me forward to the interview stage with the hiring manager.

Then her tone shifted. "Before we set up the interview," she said, a little more gently now, "I wanted to mention, the company is … well, pretty conservative. I'd recommend taming your Afro a bit before the meeting. Just to make a good impression."

Tame my Afro. As if my natural hair—curly, bouncy, alive—was something wild, something that needed to be subdued to make other people feel comfortable. My heart sank as I scrambled to process what she'd just said. The recruiter kept talking, but I couldn't hear anything over the static in my brain.

This wasn't the first time I'd been told something like that. I grew up in predominantly White neighborhoods. I worked on predominantly White teams. I'd heard the comments all my life:

- "Don't you want to straighten it for picture day?"
- "Wow, your hair feels like horse hair!"
- "Is that your real hair?"

Over the years, I'd let these comments dictate how I showed up. I straightened my hair. I toned down my outfits. I tried to make

181

myself easier to digest. But this time, something in me said no. I'd had enough, and I was tired. Not just tired of the comments but of the quiet compromises I *kept* making.

And honestly, was I ever actually fitting in?

The recruiter's words stung, but they were also a mirror. They reflected a pattern: the years I spent shrinking myself for the facade of "professionalism." All those moments I'd stayed quiet, smiled through discomfort, tried to be more palatable, kept trading authenticity for "acceptance."

Suddenly, I didn't want the role badly enough to trade pieces of myself for it.

"Thank you so much for taking the time to speak with me," I said, "but I don't think this is the right fit."

There was a pause. Then, "Oh. Are you sure? You're such a strong candidate, and this seems like a great fit."

"I'm sure."

I ended the call feeling a swirl of emotions: relief, frustration, a flicker of loss, and disappointment. But mostly, I felt proud. For the first time, I'd drawn a clear line. I wasn't going to mold myself into someone's else version of "professional" or "acceptable" just to land a job. If a company couldn't welcome me as I was, then it wasn't a place I needed to be.

That decision was a turning point. It was about more than just my hair. It was one of the first steps I took to reclaiming my identity, my values, and my voice. These days, whether I'm wearing my natural hair, rocking braids, or bright colors, I know exactly what defines me: my work, my integrity, and the impact I bring.

And you know what? I've never regretted walking away. That decision cleared space for opportunities where I never have to ask permission to show up as myself.

> ### A Little Note About Hair Discrimination
> Hair discrimination is, unfortunately, a reality many people face, particularly in professional and educational settings. If you haven't heard of the CROWN Act, it's a legislative movement aiming to end race-based hair discrimination.
>
> Created in 2019 by Dove and the Crown Coalition, in partnership with then State Senator Holly J. Mitchell of California, it seeks to guarantee "protection against discrimination based on race-based hairstyles by extending statutory protection to hair texture and protective styles such as braids, locs, twists, and knots in the workplace and public schools."

The pressure to conform often comes at a cost. Not just to your authenticity but also to your energy and creativity. How much time have you spent trying to fit into someone else's idea or definition? And how much more powerfully could you have used that time?

Flip the Script

Professionalism is about impact, not appearance. It's about your track record, not your vibe. And it's built on follow-through, integrity, thoughtfulness, and impact over time. When you strip away the dress code and corporate jargon, the question shouldn't be, "Do I seem professional?" or "Do I look the part?" The question should be, "Am I someone people trust to show up and deliver?"

If you're serious about defining professionalism on your own terms, you need a baseline. A gut check, basically. Something to measure yourself against that actually matters to you.

Ask yourself:

- Do I follow through on what I say I will?
- Do I communicate clearly, even when *(especially when)* things go sideways?
- Do I create more clarity or chaos in my team, my projects, my partnerships, etc.?
- Do I treat people with consistency and respect, regardless of title?
- Do I pursue opportunities that align with what I stand for, or do I pursue opportunities based solely on what looks impressive?

Professionalism often shows up in the small, unsexy details, because it's about integrity. That kind of professionalism—internal, deliberate, practiced—will outlast the trends, the titles, and whatever the latest version of "professional polish" happens to be. If you've ever hesitated to post a win, to show up fully, or to speak your mind at work because you didn't want to seem "too much," pause and ask yourself: "Too much of what? And according to what rules?"

It's so easy to contort yourself into what people expect … until you wake up and don't recognize what you're building anymore. Or how you're showing up.

So, here's the ask: Stop trying to look the part. Start embodying it. On your own terms. In your own voice. That's what true alignment—with yourself, your goals, your identity—actually feels like.

Breaking Down Barriers (Even When Folks Claim They Don't Exist)

If we're going to talk about professionalism, who has historically dictated it, and what change will look like, we can't ignore the elephant in the room: systemic barriers.

These are deeply ingrained norms and biases that perpetuate inequality, and they're an integral part of the systems that weren't built with everyone in mind. So, while personal empowerment is an incredibly powerful step, true progress will require more. It requires us to push back against the old-fashioned rules that limit us *and* advocate for changes that create a more inclusive, equitable playing field for everyone.

Bad News: Systemic barriers aren't dismantled overnight.

Good News: That doesn't mean we're powerless.

Small but deliberate steps can spark change that ripples outward. You might not have the authority to rewrite the company handbook or stand up to the CEO, but you absolutely have the power to challenge the small, insidious ways that systemic oppression shows up in your day-to-day work life.

It starts with the conversations you're already having. When you notice something inequitable. When you hear language that subtly (or not so subtly) enforces biases. Don't sit with the comfort. If you are in a situation where it is safe to speak up, do so.

Advocacy Without Burnout: Choose Your Moments Wisely

Anybody else feel tired, basically since 2010? And especially after the past few years (a pandemic, a ridiculous job market, tense sociopolitical climate), your girl is *tired*. Exhausted. And I know I'm not alone in this.

Earlier in the book (in the introduction), I talked about the extra labor often expected of marginalized communities, whether you're Black, a person of color, LGBTQIA+, a woman, or part of any group historically excluded from the table. Too often, we're expected to speak up for an entire community, challenge systemic barriers, and somehow stay zen while doing it. Always with a smile, never too loud, always full of grace. Meanwhile, a lot of us are just trying to make it through the workday in one piece.

And remember when we talked about burnout earlier? That absolutely applies here. Not every day will be the day to stand up and ask, "Why?" You won't always have the energy to advocate for yourself, much less for systemic change. And that's okay. This might be a spicy take, but it's one I stand by: Honor your body, your feelings, and your emotional bandwidth. There's nothing noble about depleting yourself to the point of exhaustion.

You don't have to charge into the head of HR's office demanding sweeping reforms (although if you have the energy for that, go for it). You can start by addressing smaller moments in ways that open the door for bigger discussions. For example, when someone makes an offhand comment about someone's hairstyle, my go-to question is, "What do you mean by that?" It puts the onus on them to explain and (hopefully) reflect.

It's okay to pick your battles. It's okay to let some things "slide" when your tank is on empty. Protect your mental health, your energy, and (most important) your sense of self. You're not a one-person revolution, and you don't have to be. Rest when you need to. Advocate when you can. And remember that it's perfectly valid to prioritize *yourself* in a system that's often asking for too much already.

That being said—if you want some lower-lift ways to advocate for yourself and others, here is what has helped me.

Shift the Culture Through Curiosity

Sometimes, the quietest form of advocacy is the most powerful. And sometimes, change starts by simply asking, "Why?"

- Why is this policy in place?

- Why do we do things this way?

- Why can't we do things differently?

Asking thoughtful, pointed questions can begin to challenge assumptions that others might not have even realized were there. Because these are real questions. You're not just trying to kick up dust or be difficult. You're making space for someone to justify their logic. And when the answers start to sound flimsy, people notice.

The second a room stops coasting by on habit, there's a chance for change. That's your in.

You may not have the power to rewrite the rules at the top, but you do have influence in your own sphere. You can plant seeds for the kind of cultural change that makes workplaces more equitable for yourself and for those coming after you. Once we find ways to officially interrupt the script, that's where we find momentum.

Set the Standards Before They're Set for You

Most teams don't sit down in a conference room and decide what professionalism looks like. They just absorb it from the loudest person in the room, the oldest policy on the books, or whoever has veto power in the Monday meeting. And before you know it, the standard gets baked in. Regardless of whether it makes sense or actually works.

We don't need a full-day workshop or a whiteboard to start shifting that. We can start small. When you're kicking off a new project, onboarding a contractor, or setting up a new collaboration, take five minutes to name your norms.

Here's what that might sound like:

- "I aim to respond to emails within 48 hours during the week. If it's urgent, message me on Slack."

- "I like direct feedback—don't feel like you have to sugarcoat it."

- "I block off Fridays for deep work, so I won't be in meetings unless it's time sensitive."

Then ask the other person how *they* work best. How they prefer to give and receive feedback. What helps them feel respected, trusted, and supported. Make it part of the conversation, instead of assuming you'll pick it up along the way. This is how expectations *stop* being mysterious. This is how mutual respect becomes the baseline, not a bonus. And this is how professionalism starts reflecting the people actually doing the work, not just the people approving it.

Of course, it's easier to set new standards with others than it is to examine the ones we've internalized ourselves. But that's where the deeper shift starts.

What Do *You* Value?

Unfortunately, many of us have absorbed these outdated definitions so deeply that we often don't even realize we're the ones perpetuating them now. How often have you judged someone for being "too casual" or "not taking things seriously" based on their appearance or demeanor?

This is where the real work begins, by redefining professionalism for yourself, on your terms. That's how we can begin unpacking our own biases and challenging them. Once you've named what actually matters to you, it gets a whole lot easier to move through work with clarity, integrity, and alignment. Complete the following exercise to identify what you value.

Your Turn: Define Your Professional Values

1. Write down 5–10 traits or behaviors you associate with professionalism, especially the ones that have been taught to you. Think: "always on time," "don't show too much emotion," "leave personal stuff at home," etc.

---

2. Interrogate the source. Ask yourself, "Where did these ideas come from? Was it a boss? A parent? A mentor? A cultural expectation?"

3. Then answer the question: "Do I believe this because it feels true to me or because I've been told it should?" If that question feels too tough to answer, ask yourself: "How do I feel about this quality? Do I find it relevant and important?"

4. Write your own definition of *professionalism*. What does professionalism actually look like, for you, at this stage of your life and career?

5. List five to seven values that reflect how *you* want to show up in your work. Do your best to focus less on surface-level behaviors and more on principles. Things like:

   - Integrity
   - Clarity
   - Curiosity
   - Generosity
   - Excellence without ego

   Whatever feels honest.

Once you've completed this exercise, keep your list somewhere visible. You can treat it like your own internal brand guidelines. You're not trying to use these to impress anyone; you can use them as reference points for integrity, alignment, and trust in yourself.

When the Rules Don't Apply

Ah, double standards. The rules, as written, often don't apply equally. They've been shaped over time by people in power, usually to make themselves feel more comfortable and to keep others out. So

Owning Your Version of Professionalism

historically, the definition of *professional* has been weaponized to enforce a narrow mold: straight hair, neutral tone, neutral everything. If you didn't fit, the message was clear: Reshape yourself or risk being seen as unqualified, difficult, or unprofessional.

And while the branding of this term may have softened over the years, the standards haven't shifted nearly as much as we'd like to pretend. This matters because the consequences are more than just theoretical. They affect who gets hired, who gets promoted, who gets listened to, and who gets left out of the room entirely.

Spotting the Double Standards

Bias doesn't always break down the door and announce itself. Sometimes it shows up in who gets described as "strategic" versus "too blunt." Sometimes it's in a manager's face when you walk into a meeting with box braids and a bold lip. Sometimes it's in the performance review where your confidence is seen as "a little aggressive."

Let's break it down. A casual email from one person might read as confident. From someone else, careless. Tattoos can be "cool" on one person and "inappropriate" on another. A hoodie on a White man in tech signals brilliance. A hoodie on a Black woman? Suddenly there are concerns about professionalism.

These inconsistencies shape how people are perceived, how feedback is delivered, and who's trusted to lead.

So ... What Do We Do About It?

You get to define the rules you live by. And that includes recognizing when the system was built to keep you guessing and staying clear-eyed when the game is rigged.

Don't feel like you have to walk into every meeting with a protest sign. But you also get to figure out what professional means on your own terms and show up like you mean it. Not to impress but to take up space.

That might look different depending on the room. Sometimes the tool is data. Sometimes it's humor. Sometimes it's a well-placed pause or a direct question. Other times, it's the way you say no, the way you dress, or the silence you choose to keep. You're still you. You're just choosing the right tool for the moment.

So, rock the braids. Wear the bright, unconventional outfit. Let your tone be sharp, your standards high, and your work impossible to ignore. The right people will be paying attention. The rest are still rewriting the employee handbook like it's 2004. This is strategy. You already belong in the room. Now you get to decide how you show up in it.

Once you stop performing the version of "professional" that people expect, you'll start getting reactions. Some curious. Some supportive. Some clearly rooted in someone else's discomfort. That's where the next test begins.

Handling Pushback Like a Pro (Without Losing Your Cool)

Redefining professionalism isn't always met with applause. Sometimes, it's met with skepticism, microaggressions, or just plain old resistance. And while it would be lovely and amazing to exist in a world where our individuality and diverse backgrounds are celebrated, that's not always reality.

Pushback is inevitable. Some people cling to their old rules like a security blanket, whether it's because they genuinely believe in them or because those rules have always worked in their favor (usually the latter). So, what do you do when someone side-eyes your braids or questions the credibility of your experience because you didn't walk a traditional career path?

Master the Art of the Redirect

Sometimes, people's biases seep out in the form of backhanded compliments, offhand remarks, or those "just curious" questions. You don't have to take it upon yourself to swallow the awkwardness or over-explain yourself. Redirect it. Refocus the energy. Shift the discomfort to the person who *should* be feeling it: the one asking the inappropriate questions or sharing their unsolicited opinions.

When someone says something that veers off-course, I keep it simple: acknowledge; then pivot. For example: "That's an interesting perspective on my tattoos, but let's get back to the meeting. About that Q3 rollout plan ..."

You don't have to clap back. You don't have to be theatrical. Just steer the conversation with purpose. That's power. And *that* is professionalism.

Set Clear Boundaries

There's a difference between curiosity and judgment. Honestly, I hardly have time for either, but you're under no obligation to entertain the latter. If someone crosses a line, don't hesitate to draw one of your own. Some people will like to treat your identity like small talk. "Where are you *really* from?" "Wow, that's a ... bold outfit!" "Do you always wear your hair like that?"

In my opinion, these aren't genuine questions. They're surveillance disguised as curiosity. When you set boundaries with confidence, they become self-enforcing. People either rise to meet you or quietly disqualify themselves.

When people make inappropriate comments or ask inappropriate questions, my go-to response is: "Let's focus on the project, not [personal commentary/my outfit/the way I look]."

That one sentence has saved me hours of emotional labor. You don't owe anyone access to your interior life just because they're confused by your exterior. But you *do* owe yourself a professional environment that doesn't drain you.

Prepare, Document, and Advocate

Sometimes the discomfort will continue to build. It will creep from offhanded comments to work culture. Some people might double down on their resistance. They'll come prepared with passive-aggressive comments, thinly veiled critiques, and microaggressions. You're holding up a mirror to people's biases, and that tends to make folks uncomfortable. If the pushback escalates into something that is more systemic, or something that is beginning to put your job or psychological safety at risk, keep a record. Your best protection is a paper trail.

So how do you handle it?

First, *expect it*. You don't need to live in constant anticipation of conflict, but pushback comes in waves. The first might be subtle: a comment about how "times are a'changing" or "things were simpler when [*fill in the blank*]." By the time the third or fourth wave comes around, you'll have the receipts.

I always tell my friends, "Document first; confront later." Get it in writing. Not because you're planning to go nuclear, but because clarity is our friend in these situations. Vibes are not admissible in an HR investigation (unfortunately).

Write down what was said, when, and who was there. Take screenshots. Flag patterns. Collect emails. And if you need to escalate, show up with facts. But also keep track of your wins, your contributions, and any feedback that highlights your impact. The numbers don't lie.

Advocating for yourself can look like quiet preparation. It doesn't have to look like a loud confrontation. Sometimes it looks like telling the truth, calmly, with backup and receipts.

Second, *don't take the bait.* Not every comment or critique deserves your energy. If someone is committed to misunderstanding you, no amount of reasoning will change their mind. Control what you can, and let the rest roll off your shoulders (or try to; deep breaths do help).

And finally, *stay grounded in your "why."* Why are you invested in redefining professionalism for yourself? Why does this matter to you? Reconnecting with that purpose, especially on tough days, can remind you that the pushback is temporary but the change you're advocating for is worth it.

Protect Your Energy

Not everyone will come around, no matter how compelling your argument is. Some people are *deeply* invested in maintaining the status quo. They cling to outdated norms like a comfort blanket. You could spend *years* trying to convince them to see you differently, to loosen their grip on the way things "have always been." Or you could reroute your energy toward people who are already leaning into the future with you.

That's the decision I made. I don't spend my days chasing prospects who flinch at my hand tattoos or wonder if my braids are "too much." I spend my days with clients who care about the work. Who trust my voice, respect my values, and couldn't care less about what's on my wrist as long as I deliver. (Which I do.)

Trying to prove yourself to people who've already written you off, and decided they won't see you, is a full-time job, and it doesn't come with benefits. The real opportunity lives elsewhere, in rooms where your presence doesn't need to be justified and in conversations that move forward because you're in them, not in spite of it. You are allowed to opt out of "performing." You are allowed to build a career that reflects your values, your voice, and your style. You are allowed to protect your energy like it's the most valuable thing you own, because it is.

There's no single way to redefine professionalism, but there is a through line: integrity, impact, and intention. The rest is your call. So, take up space. Set your own terms. Let the "That's unprofessional!" crowd keep their bylaws. You've got your own handbook now.

And if anyone has a problem with that, they can take it up with the tattoos.

Takeaways

- Professionalism is a practice, not a costume. What actually earns trust isn't your outfit or tone of voice. It's how you show up when things get messy. Do you deliver? Do you communicate clearly? Do you lead with intention? That's the kind of professionalism that holds up over time.
- Choose your tools on purpose. Each moment will call for different kinds of advocacy. Sometimes your power is in a redirect, a question, a firm boundary, or a quiet refusal to play around. You get to decide what you bring into the room and what you leave at the door.
- Stop chasing the people who need convincing. There will always be someone clinging to the "old way." Let them. Your job is to do meaningful work with people who get it, not twist yourself into something they find palatable. The more you contort yourself to win over people who've already written you off, the more energy you waste trying to prove your right to exist.

Chapter 14

Delegating and Getting Out of the Way

When I hired my first part-time assistant, I was thrilled (at least on paper). Finally, someone to help lighten the load! Someone to handle the recurring to-dos while I focused on growth.

Except that's not what happened.

I clung to my to-do list like a lifeline. I triple-checked every spreadsheet she touched. I micromanaged *her* management of my inbox. And I ended up doing most of the work myself, which defeated the whole purpose. I didn't trust her, but that wasn't because of her competence. It was *all* about my control. I was convinced that I could do everything faster, better, cleaner. And if I was going to end up fixing it later, why delegate it in the first place?

Then came my breaking point. My client load tripled, my inbox became unmanageable, and the cracks started to show. I was forgetting things, missing deadlines, and running at full speed just to stay behind. So, I hired a full-time assistant. To be clear, I hadn't suddenly become good at delegating. I just didn't have a choice. I *needed* help. And that's where things shifted.

My new assistant was all in. She was competent, organized, detail-oriented, and calm under pressure. And she kept asking for more work. About a month in, she started pointing out that I was still doing the tasks I'd hired her to own, and that's when it hit me.

I wasn't being a good leader. Or a good founder. I was being my own bottleneck and my own worst enemy.

Bit by bit, I started handing things over. A client file here, a draft review there. And she didn't drop the ball or miss things, like I feared she would. She leveled things up. And in doing so, she taught me something so simple and game-changing: You can't scale *anything* if you're still clutching every little piece of it.

Giving Up Control

Delegation is hard for a reason. It demands a level of trust and self-awareness that most high achievers aren't exactly trained for. It challenges you to let go of your grip on perfection and to let go of your belief that only you can do it right. It's more than just handing off tasks. You're giving up control, influence, and sometimes even credit. And if you've built something from the ground up, that loss can feel personal. The first time you watch someone else take the wheel on something you used to do yourself, your brain might scream, "They're going to wreck it!"

Whether you're running your own business, building a career you've poured your soul into, or managing a team, delegation can feel like you're giving away a piece of yourself. Your work is your "baby," right? And it can feel damn near impossible to trust someone else to care for it with the same attention, respect, and diligence that you do. It can feel reckless or like you're asking for it to fall apart.

But doing it all yourself is its own kind of failure. While you're over here polishing the perfect spreadsheet, obsessively checking your own inbox, and micromanaging every moving part, the strategic work is going untouched. The bigger vision is gathering dust. The work *only you can do* is sitting on the back burner while you're buried in stuff someone else could've handled hours ago.

Eventually, the weight adds up. You burn out. You stall. Maybe you start to resent your work, your team, or even yourself. And by the time you realize you've become the bottleneck, the damage is already visible—in missed opportunities, delayed growth … and way too many tabs open.

Delegation is a leadership muscle. And like any muscle, you build it by practicing, not by waiting until you "feel ready."

Which brings us to the first move: building your Let Go Plan.

The Let Go Plan (aka, Your Opportunity Cost Calendar)

Let's stop treating delegation like a luxury and start treating it like a strategy.

In your notebook or a spreadsheet, make three columns as shown in Table 14.1.

Then go through your weekly work and log everything you're currently doing that someone else could feasibly take on. Include administrative work, but also look at other areas:

- Operations
- Content prep
- Scheduling
- Finance
- Client management
- Onboarding
- Follow-ups

Table 14.1   Let Go Plan

Tasks	Hours Per Week	What That Time *Could* Be Used For

Once you have your list, ask yourself the following questions:

- *What's the true cost of me doing this myself?* Remember, cost is more than just time. It's energy, attention, decision-making bandwidth, and creative focus. If something takes you 90 minutes, but it leaves you too drained to tackle the strategic work that actually moves your business forward, that's expensive. The true cost might be missed growth opportunities, slower project timelines, mental fatigue, staying stuck in the weeds while your vision stalls out ... the list goes on and on.

- *What am I missing out on while I spend time here?* Every "yes" comes with an invisible "no." The two hours you spend on a task you could've delegated are two hours you didn't spend pitching a dream client or thinking deeply about the next stage of your career. What higher-leverage work is going untouched while you're stuck doing something that could live on someone else's plate?

- *What is the ROI of letting go?* When I talk about ROI in this context, I'm not just referring to money saved or time freed up. I'm talking about momentum and headspace. It's about finally having the margin to be thoughtful instead of reactive. Delegation is an *investment*. The return might look like this:

  - More consistent delivery.
  - Better- or higher-quality output.
  - Increased revenue.
  - The sheer relief of knowing things are being handled without your constant supervision.

When you offload the *right* things, your capacity expands—and so does your business/career. Because you're trading more than just your time—you're trading capacity, energy, and strategic focus. And more often than not, we waste that energy holding onto tasks that someone else could do just as well. Or better!

And yes, you might still do it faster. But faster isn't the goal if you're doing 100 different things at once and showing up half-present for all of them. Think of this as your Let Go Plan—the first step in building something that doesn't collapse the second you take a breath. Congratulations! You're reclaiming your bandwidth.

So, what exactly should stay on your plate? Let's think about the stuff only you can do and how to figure out what you should be ready to pass along.

What Only You Can Do (and What You're Just Really Good At)

Delegation gets a whole lot easier when we can be honest about the difference between what's truly ours to hold and what's just hanging around out of muscle memory, ego, or pride. Here's how I think about it:

- If it absolutely requires my voice, my brain, my lived experience, or my relationships, then it probably stays on my plate.

- If I'm just good at it because I've been doing it forever, that's a maybe. Maybe it's time to train someone else or let it go.

This is where so many founders and leaders get tripped up. They confuse "I'm good at this" with "No one else can do this." Those aren't the same. I'm great at building pitch decks. I can build landing pages in my sleep. I know how to manage influencers like a pro. But does that mean I should still be the one doing those things, all the time? Absolutely not. Because being good at something doesn't mean it needs your fingerprints on it forever. And your zone of excellence shouldn't always be your zone of ownership.

Here's how I separate what stays, what gets handed off, and what needs a system:

- *Keep the stuff only you can do.* Founder-level moves. Vision-defining decisions. Final sign-off on brand and voice. Anything that pulls directly from your creative side, strategic lens, or your unique lived experiences. If it shapes the culture, impacts the direction, or would go sideways without your perspective or oversight, that's yours.

- *Delegate the stuff you're great at but don't need to own.* You've probably mastered it. Might even enjoy it. Doesn't matter. This is the stuff you can pass off with a little training or an SOP. Think project management, internal documentation, process building, etc. If someone else can do 90% of it and you can refine the last 10%, pass the baton.

- *Systematize the stuff that's clogging your calendar.* This is the "ugh" work. The stuff you dread, delay, or distract yourself from. The administrative work, repeatable steps. Make it a checklist, turn it into a template, automate it, outsource it. Just stop keeping it on your plate out of guilt or habit.

When you're clear on what belongs to you and what doesn't, delegation stops feeling like a risk and starts looking like a smart investment. One that buys you space, clarity, and time to lead the business you're actually trying to build.

When You Don't Let Go

It's easy to blame the systems or the team or the workload. But sometimes the real reason things aren't moving is less complicated than that. Sometimes the part slowing everything down is *you*.

Not because you're lazy or because you don't care. But I'd bet good money that you've built a system where *everything* filters through you. You're overcapacity, overstimulated, and overstretched. And yet you're still the one reviewing all the email copy, tweaking the slide deck, and holding back approvals because you need "more time to review." Meanwhile your team is circling in a holding pattern, unsure whether to move forward or wait for you to magically become available.

Most bottlenecks creep in quietly, wearing the disguise of being "thorough" or "involved" or "just really passionate about quality." But if everything depends on you, then everything bottlenecks at you. That's a house of cards. Here's how to check yourself:

- Are you the last step in too many processes?

- Are you redoing work instead of giving real feedback?

- Are you constantly "in the loop" but still feel behind on everything?

- Are decisions, deliverables, and progress constantly waiting on *you*?

When this happens, you slow down projects, but you're also eroding trust. Your team stops making decisions without you because you've trained them to assume their decisions won't stick. You become the person they're all waiting on, even when you didn't mean to be. And the longer it goes unaddressed, the more your team learns to wait instead of lead.

So, if you've already made a Let Go Plan, if you already know what's yours to own and what isn't, this is the moment you stop letting your involvement be the excuse. Let people do what you hired them to do. Let systems hold what they're supposed to hold. And if you're still scared to let go, remember: You're holding back the business.

Trusting Your Team Means Trusting Your Judgment

If you're second-guessing your team at every turn, you're also second-guessing the person who hired them: you.

You picked these people. You interviewed them, scanned their portfolios, dug through their résumés, asked a handful of "what would you do if …" questions, and decided they had what it takes. So, if you're struggling to hand things off now, is the issue with their competency level? Or is it about your comfort with letting go?

Hiring is a skill. And just like any other skill, you get better with practice. If you've made the wrong hire in the past, welcome to the club. Maybe they looked great on paper. Maybe they said all the right things in the interview. Maybe they were great … just not what you needed. Whatever the reason, cool! You learned something. That's how you sharpen your judgment.

What makes hiring *easier* (and delegation less painful) is having a process built around your actual needs and your company's goals, not just someone else's best practices.

How I Hire

Here are some things I do when I hire. Feel free to use, tweak, and steal them:

- I tell people, upfront, how I work—how I give feedback, what I expect, and what I appreciate. Saves everyone time, especially me.

- I send interview questions ahead of time. I want each candidate at their best, not just their fastest.

- I ask people how *they* like to be managed, how they learn, and how they collaborate. There's no perfect answer—I just want to

---

> know what kind of support they'll need and how they'll mesh
> with the team.
>
> - I ask direct questions about work style, red flags, and how they
>   prefer to receive (and give) feedback.

Scaling Trust, One Step at a Time

Trust can start small. You don't have to throw your most high-stakes projects at someone new on day one. Let trust be earned through action, not assumed from the jump.

Start with something low stakes, give clear direction, and let people show you what they're capable of. Inbox triage. Research. Scheduling. A recurring task you've already stopped giving your full attention to. Pick one thing you're holding out of habit, not because it actually requires your expertise. Then let it go. Fully. Let them own it and let the results speak for themselves.

Trust takes time. So set boundaries that make sense for where you're at. When I first hired my full-time assistant, I kept client-facing work or sensitive tasks to myself because it gave me peace of mind. I started with the backend work. Over time, as my assistant gained confidence and I stopped white-knuckling every project, her scope expanded.

Delegation is a skill. So is knowing when to step back. One day you'll open Slack and realize a whole category of work hasn't crossed your desk in weeks. Not because it disappeared, but because your team handled it cleanly, quietly, and without needing to ask for a dozen approvals.

That is the return. You get hours back on your calendar, but you also get back mental space you didn't even realize you were renting out. That's what trust buys you. More focus, fewer bottlenecks, and a team that feels empowered (instead of babysat). Trust scales when it's mutual—when your team trusts you to lead and you trust them to get the damn thing done.

Learning Through Hires (and Misfires)

Remember when I said that delegation is a leadership muscle? It will get stronger with repetition, failure, and a little soreness along the way.

Some hires will absolutely crush it. Others will ghost you mid-project, send a deliverable that makes your eye twitch, or need more hand-holding than you realistically have time to give. This doesn't mean you're a bad leader. This doesn't mean you're bad at hiring. Every misstep gives you sharper instincts for the next round.

Here are some things to look for and log:

- Did they overpromise in the interview and underdeliver on the job? Look back at what you might have missed in their answers.

- Did you set vague expectations? Reevaluate and rework your onboarding checklist or your training documents. If you're winging it, they will too.

- Did you delegate too fast or too much? Note the tipping point and try adjusting your pacing next time.

Delegation will always involve a little risk. You're handing over a piece of something you've built, something you care about. There's always the chance that it won't go as you imagined. But your ability to navigate that, recover, reset, and try again, is what makes you a stronger operator and leader. Delegation isn't just about trusting other people. It's about trusting yourself to handle the fallout if things don't go perfectly.

Takeaways

- Delegation is a leadership skill, not a luxury. The sooner you treat it like part of your actual job (not something you'll get around to), the more bandwidth, clarity, and creative focus you reclaim.
- If everything runs through you, everything slows down because of you. Bottleneck behavior is just fear in disguise. And the more you cling to every detail, the more you block momentum.
- Your job isn't to do it all. Your job is to build something that runs without your fingerprints on every single thing. It's okay to start small, set clear expectations, and let people earn your trust through action.

Chapter 15

Your Career Is Not Your Identity

There's a moment we've all experienced—at a dinner party, networking event, or maybe even a first date—when the inevitable question drops:

"So, what do you do?"

And just like that, the entire weight of your existence gets boiled down to a job title.

It's a simple question, but it's doing a lot of work. It's not asking *who* you are. It's asking what you produce. What you're known for. What gives you value. And if you've internalized that long enough, it starts to shape the way you see yourself too. You start to believe that your career isn't just something you do. It's who you are.

That belief is a trap. I'm not trying to say that work can't be meaningful. It can! It can be purpose-driven, energizing, even central to your life. But it can't be *everything*. It's not designed to fulfill every part of you. It's one slice of the pie, and no, it doesn't get to be the biggest one.

Fulfillment (real, grounded, lasting fulfillment) is layered. It's centered on looking at your life as a whole and seeing all the ways it can grow, stretch, and surprise you, both inside and outside of work. And it happens when we create a life that doesn't orbit entirely around work. It's the laughter over dinner with friends, the freedom to rest without guilt, the thrill of learning something new. The kind of joy that doesn't come with a performance review or a paycheck.

You are more than your email signature, your LinkedIn headline, or the side hustle you've poured your weekends into. You are allowed—*expected*, even—to have parts of your identity that exist outside of what you do for a living. And reclaiming those parts is how you start to build a life that feels whole.

When Work Becomes the Center of the Universe

At one point in my career, I was so ashamed of my job title ("I'm *just* a marketing specialist") that I shied away from conversations about work. I felt lesser-than. Lesser-than who, though, I had no idea. To be completely honest, this is an area I still deeply struggle with. Always have. Which I think makes me uniquely positioned to tell you how to *avoid* doing what I do.

Somewhere along the way, with my business Verbatim, I started to notice something unsettling. Whenever people asked me how *I* was doing, I answered with updates about the business.

"How's it going?"

"Oh, great! Just signed a new client last week."

"What's new with you?"

"Busy busy! I'm wrapping up this huge project at work, and it's been intense."

It was like I couldn't separate myself from my work. Partly because I love it so much and partly because of how I perceive success. The scariest part is that I didn't even realize I was doing it at first. My personal life, my hobbies, my sense of self, had all taken a backseat to the business. Verbatim was who I *was*, not just what I *did*.

It wasn't until I hit a particularly rough patch (*hello, burnout, my old friend*) that I had to take a hard look at what was happening.

My entire sense of worth was tied to the success (or perceived success) of my business. If Verbatim was thriving, I was thriving. If things got rocky, I was a failure as a business owner *and* as a person. And let me tell you, that's a terrifying amount of pressure to put on yourself.

When your career becomes your identity, the stakes are *impossibly* high. Every setback is personal. Every criticism cuts deeper. And every moment when you're not actively achieving something can feel like you're falling behind. It's exhausting.

The mindset is especially dangerous in the world of portfolio careers, freelancing, and entrepreneurship. When you're your own boss, your work feels like an extension of you. But work isn't the sum total of who you are. Your value isn't tied to your productivity or your output, no matter how much society and social media try to tell us otherwise.

The Multidimensional You

So ... who are you outside of work? If that question makes you feel a little uncomfortable, or completely panicked, that's okay! It's not an easy one to answer, especially when you've spent so much time and energy building a career that demands your full attention.

Let's start with the basics:

- What lights you up outside of work? Hobbies, interests, guilty pleasures. What's on your "I'd do this for fun" list?
- Who are the people you love? What do you love about them? Friends, family, partners. What do they bring to your life that work never could?
- What values drive you that have nothing to do with your job? Community, curiosity, creativity. What are things that you care about deeply?

Your Career Is Not Your Identity

Write these things down. Seriously. Get a notebook, a whiteboard, open your Notes app, or use the back of a receipt if you have to. The goal here is not to "figure it all out" in one sitting. It's to remind yourself that there's more to you than your title or to-do list.

Remembering Who You Are (Outside of Work)

Sometimes the best way to rediscover your balance is by finding joy in something that has *nothing* to do with work at all.

Which sounds simple enough. But if you're used to measuring your worth by your output, or if you're like me and you've spent years training your brain to associate achievement with validation, then doing something *just because it makes you happy* can feel wildly unproductive. Maybe even a little uncomfortable. But joy—real, sustaining, centering joy—rarely lives in your inbox. It's what reminds us that we're a whole person, not just a job description with a to-do list and KPIs. And for me, that reminder came with chalky hands and sore forearms.

One of the biggest projects I'd ever pitched fell apart at the eleventh hour. Weeks of late nights, strategy calls, proposal decks, and back-and-forth emails—completely wiped out by a single message: "We've decided to go in another direction." It knocked the wind out of me. I'd poured so much time, energy, and, if I'm being honest, my self-worth into making it happen.

When it all collapsed, I just sat there staring at my laptop like it owed me an explanation. I needed space to process the loss. Not through another strategy call, but by doing something that had absolutely nothing to do with work.

Months earlier, I'd tried indoor bouldering with a friend and loved it. Told myself I'd be back every week, but life got in the way. But now, climbing felt like exactly the kind of full-body focus I needed.

So, I went. I rented shoes, borrowed some chalk, and started showing up at Alta a couple of times a week, armed with my AirPods and a playlist that bounced between heavy metal, classical, and Kendrick Lamar. For the first time in weeks, my brain finally shut up. When you're 10 feet off the ground, gripping a hold the size of a coin, you're not thinking about client meetings or emails. You're just present, in the moment, trying to climb higher. Trying not to fall. It was exhilarating, humbling, and exactly what I needed to get out of my head.

At first, it felt a little irresponsible to be climbing while my business still felt shaky. But stepping away gave me something I hadn't realized was missing: clarity, control, and a dose of humility (because nothing keeps you grounded like falling in front of strangers). And when I turned back to work each day, I felt lighter. Sharper. The pressure I'd been carrying around didn't feel quite so heavy. The outcome of that project still stung, but it didn't define me or my business.

I'm not just an entrepreneur. I'm a climber (amateur, but enthusiastic), a pianist, a writer, and a person who occasionally blasts heavy metal while dangling off plastic rocks. And somehow, tapping back into that part of myself made me better at everything else. Sometimes, the best way to rediscover your balance is by finding joy in something that has nothing to do with work at all. For me, that joy came in the form of chalky hands, bruised knees, and a few well-deserved breaks.

How to Figure Out Who You Are Outside of Work

Okay, so you're convinced: Your career shouldn't be your whole identity. But figuring out who you are outside of work can be overwhelming and confusing, especially if you've let your career take up the spotlight for years. It's like meeting yourself for the first time, but instead of a simple, "Nice to meet you," you're trying to answer questions like, "What brings you joy?" and "Who am I, really?" Cue the existential spiral, thanks.

First things first, you're not going to answer these questions overnight. And that's okay! Figuring out who you are is not a pop quiz. It's a process. Let yourself feel curious, not pressured. When you've spent years measuring your time, energy, and self-worth in career milestones, it's easy for your identity to flatten into just one thing: work. Even when you know intellectually that you're more than your job, it can still *feel* like work is the default setting. It's where your time goes. It's what people ask about. It's what gets rewarded.

The work matters, but the other parts of your life do too. So, let's do a visual gut check.

Complete a Visual Gut Check

1. Draw a circle and divide it into sections, like a pie chart, with each slice representing a different area of your life: careers, relationships, creativity, hobbies, health, rest, learning, spirituality, community, whatever fits *your* world right now.

2. Shade each slice to reflect how much of your time and energy actually goes into it.

3. Draw a second circle. Same categories, but this time, shade them in based on how you *want* your time and energy to be distributed.

4. Compare the two circles. What's missing? What's overgrown? What's been getting your leftover energy instead of your full attention?

My Visual Gut Check

When I first did this exercise, work took up nearly half of my "current" pie. Not just because I run a business, but because I let it bleed into everything: my mornings, my weekends, my conversations, my sense of self. The rest of the pie was just slivers:

- *Exercise*, which I barely made time for.

- *Family*, which meant my fiancé, pets, mom, brother, sister-in-law, and nieces—but rarely all at once, and rarely with the kind of presence I wanted.

- *Movies*, which I adore but had started guilting myself out of watching, as if I needed to earn the right to watch them.

- And one last unlabeled slice: *leftovers*—whatever was left after everything else.

Then I drew the second pie. The one I actually wanted. And just seeing it clarified *so* much. I didn't want to cut out work. I love what I do. But I wanted it to take up less space. I wanted to watch movies without thinking about what else I "should" be doing. To take long walks with my fiancé and just listen. To spend time with my nieces without mentally scanning my inbox. To move my body and lift weights because it makes me feel grounded, not just because it "offsets" my stress.

The difference between those two pies was how I spent my time. But it was also how I saw myself. The first one told a story I didn't even realize I'd been living: that work was the most important, most worthy part of me. And everything else could just fit around it. The second pie shifted the narrative. It reminded me that joy, rest, connection, creativity weren't just extras. They're not things I have to earn after being productive. They're part of what makes me, *me*.

So, if you're staring at your own pie and realizing it's a little lopsided, good!

How to Regain Your Balance

After completing the Visual Gut Check exercise, it is time to figure out what actually lights you up outside of work, without overthinking it.

Step 1: Revisit What Used to Make You Happy

Remember when you were a kid and you just did things because they were fun? Not because they made you money, looked good on Instagram, or fit into some grand plan? What were some of those things?

Those activities often give you clues about what still excites you. For me, it was writing stories, painting and coloring, and exploring the outdoors.

If you're drawing a blank, try this: Give yourself permission to be curious. Think of one thing you've always wanted to try—whether it's salsa dancing, learning to knit, or learning how to whittle (highly recommend, by the way)—and just go for it. No pressure to be good at it. Just explore.

Step 2: Pay Attention to What Energizes You

Think about the last time you truly felt energized or in the zone. What were you doing? Who were you with? Maybe it was a solo walk that cleared your head. Or maybe you're like my friend Gabby, and you get in the zone when you have a new LEGO™ set.

Energizing moments often live in the things we overlook because they're not inherently, or obviously, productive. But they're worth paying attention to! They show you what you naturally gravitate toward, what fills you up instead of draining you, and what you'd keep doing just for fun, even if no one ever saw or praised it.

Step 3: Experiment Without Expectations

Here's the fun part: Try new things just to see how they feel. Sign up for a class, pick up a book about something random, or take a solo trip to a place you've never been. For me, I always loved movies (watching them, analyzing them, talking about them, dreaming about them, normal stuff), but I had never even considered being a film festival judge. When I finally tried it, it was a random decision on a Sunday afternoon. I applied, got selected, and now I've been doing it for years.

You don't have to become an expert. Reconnect with the joy of doing something just for you.

Step 4: Reflect and Iterate

As you explore and try new things (or old interests), take mental or physical notes. Think about why it felt meaningful or exciting, and don't be afraid to pivot. If you don't enjoy something, move on. You don't have to nail down a definitive identity right now; focus on learning more about what makes you tick.

Okay, so now you've done the reflection. You've poked at old interests, paid attention to what lights you up, maybe even tried a few things just for fun. But what do you *do* with all of that? You build a life around it. And one of the easiest ways to start is by creating a nonwork bucket list.

Step 5: Create Your Non-work Bucket List

Think of your non-work bucket list as a space to collect the ideas, passions, and daydreams that surfaced in the steps above. The ones you always push aside for "someday." The things that have *nothing* to do with your career path and everything to do with who you are as a human being.

Your list can include big dreams, tiny joys, random curiosities … whatever interests you. The only rule is that it can't be related to work. This is about feeding the other parts of you—the playful, curious, connected, creative parts that might be running on fumes. Consider it an act of rebellion against a culture that glorifies burnout and busyness. This list should be unapologetically about *you*.

Here are some tips to get you started:

- *Dream big.* What's a life experience you've always wanted but never prioritized? Write it down.

- *Dream small.* Not everything has to be grand. Maybe it's having a lazy Sunday with a stack of novels or mastering the perfect latte at home.

- *Get specific.* Vague goals are harder to chase. Instead of writing, "Travel more," write down something like, "Spend a week in Kyoto during cherry blossom season (*and bring Brianna along*)."

- *Involve your loved ones.* Some dreams are even better when you share them! Plan a road trip with your best friend or a night under the stars with your kids.

Here is some of my list for inspiration:

- Visit every national park in the United States.
- Go on a solo trip to Japan.
- Host an epic destination birthday with my and my partner's favorite people.
- Take a luxury train trip through Europe.
- Attend the Cannes Film Festival.
- Publish a novel (check!).
- Try bouldering outdoors.
- Volunteer at a wildlife rescue.
- Plant a garden (or at least keep a single herb alive for more than week).
- Learn to play the guitar.

- Become fluent in Chinese.

- See the Northern Lights in Iceland.

- Learn how to DJ.

- Learn how to surf (maybe learn how to swim first?).

Now it's your turn. Think of this as your permission slip to dream, explore, and play. Let yourself lean into the things that excite you or just make you smile. It doesn't have to be groundbreaking or Insta-worthy. It just has to help you create a life that feels full, vibrant, and meaningful, no matter what's happening at work.

Wrapping It All Up: You Are Enough

Let's end with a reminder that you might need to hear: *You are enough*. Right now. Exactly as you are. Not because of what you do, how much money you make, or how many followers you have, but because you exist. Your work is a huge part of you, sure, but it's not all of you. And the more you lean into the fullness of your identity, the more vibrant, meaningful, and fulfilling your life will become.

So, the next time someone asks, "What do you do?" feel free to tell them about your job. Be proud of it. But don't stop there. Maybe tell them about the karaoke nights, the plant obsession, the book you can't put down, or the dream you're working on outside of work. Show them, and yourself, that you are so much more than your career.

Takeaways

- Your career is a chapter in your life, not your entire story. It might be a meaningful chapter, even a long whole, but it's not the whole book. Letting work define your entire identity puts too much pressure on one part of your life to do all the heavy lifting.
- Fulfillment comes from a rich, multidimensional life. That can include climbing the corporate ladder, but it also comes from building a life with depth and variety. The more dimensions you explore, the more whole your life will feel.
- Reclaiming your identity starts with curiosity. You don't need to have it all figured out. You just need to be willing to ask yourself, "What else is here?" The more you follow those questions—into hobbies, memories, places, even daydreams—the more you remember who you are outside of what you do.

Conclusion

So here we are. At the end of the book, but not the end of your story.

If I've done my job, you're walking away with more than just strategies and frameworks. You're leaving with a fire in your chest and a reminder: You belong in every space you walk into. Not because someone gave you a seat, but because you deserve one.

We've covered a lot. Imposter syndrome, resilience, career pivots, invisible income, unsexy systems, detaching your identity and self-worth from your career. We've talked about what it means to be the kind of person who builds a career, a business, a life, without a script. We don't have to wait for permission. We can learn, reinvent, fail forward, and keep going.

And we don't have to play the game better. We can opt out of the game entirely and build something real instead.

Your Story Is Worth Telling

Even if it's still in progress. Even if it's messy, nonlinear, or not tied up with a shiny little bow. Especially then. And it's worth telling not because it's perfect but because it's yours. Your story isn't just about what you do, but how you move through the world. It's about the risks you took, the no's you said, the boundaries you set, the creative detours.

That's the good stuff.

So don't wait until you *feel* impressive. Share your story now. Use it to connect, to lead, to make someone else feel less alone. The last thing the world needs is another highlight reel. What we need is real people building real things, in real time.

Taking Up Space *Is* the Work

If you've ever felt the pressure to shrink, conform, and play by rules that weren't written with you in mind, welcome. I see you, and you're not alone because I've been there too. But we don't need anyone's permission to be here. We're already here, and we're already building. Every time we show up as our full, unapologetic selves, we're carving out space for ourselves and others.

Taking up space isn't easy. Sometimes it feels like swimming upstream or climbing Mount Everest (or in my case, doing any hike, ever). It's exhausting. But it's a radical act of defiance and self-love. It's how we advocate for ourselves, shift the narrative, and reshape the table for those coming up behind us. It's how things change and how we stop editing ourselves into oblivion.

This Is Just the Beginning

If you're reading this, you've already done the hard part. You've chosen to step into your power.

Maybe you're mid-pivot, mid-burnout, mid-renaissance, or rebuilding from scratch, again. Wherever you're at, congratulations! That's not failure. That's growth. Whatever comes next, I hope you walk into it with more clarity, with more confidence, and with way less tolerance for anything that doesn't serve you.

A Final Note

As we close out this book, here's what I want you to remember:

You don't need to earn your space. You don't need to wait for the right title, follower count, degree, or nod of approval. You get to show up as you are, build what you want, and change your mind along the way.

So, claim your space. Tell your story, loudly, unapologetically, on your own damn terms. Take up more room than you think you're allowed. Build your career, business, and life in a way that feels true to who you are, not the version someone else expects.

And when you look back on this chapter of your life, I hope you'll see how far you've come, how much you've grown, and how powerful your story really is.

This isn't a conclusion. It's a call to action.

Let's get to work.

Chapter 1: Understanding Imposter Syndrome

1. Martin R. Huecker, Jacob Shreffler, Patrick T. McKeny, and David Davis, *National Library of Medicine* (Treasure Island, FL: StatPearls Publishing, 2023).
2. Lean In, *The State of Black Women in Corporate America* (2020), leanin.org.
3. Author interview with April Little, December 17, 2024.

Chapter 2: Acknowledging Your Worth and Owning Your Impact

1. Author interview with April Little, December 17, 2024.

Chapter 4: Building Your Circle: Mentors, Sponsors, and the Power of Community

1. Author interview with Tobi Oluwole, January 14, 2025.

Chapter 5: Deciding If a Portfolio Career Is Right for You

1. Author interview with Aleah Roseen, January 9, 2025.

Chapter 6: Building a Purposeful Portfolio Career

1. Author interview with Linda Le, December 5, 2024.
2. Author interview with Sharayah "Ray" Wilson, February 3, 2025.

Chapter 7: Designing a Career That Grows with You

1. Author interview with Elfried Samba, December 13, 2024.
2. Author interview with Morgan J. Ingram, December 10, 2024.

Chapter 8: Avoiding Burnout

1. World Health Organization, "Burn-out an 'Occupational Phenomenon,'" *International Classification of Diseases*, May 28, 2019, https://www.who.int/news/item/28-05-2019-burn-out-an-occupational-phenomenon-international-classification-of-diseases.
2. Author interview with Elfried Samba, December 13, 2024.
3. Author interview with Elfried Samba, December 13, 2024.

Index